W9-AYM-804

3439

THE GOOD OLD DAYS

AMERICA IN THE '40s & '50s

THE GOOD OLD DAYS

AMERICA IN THE '40s & '50s

By the Editors of Time-Life Books

Time-Life Books, Alexandria, Virginia

Time-Life Books is a division of Time Life Inc.

TIME-LIFE CUSTOM PUBLISHING
VICE PRESIDENT and PUBLISHER: Terry Newell
Project Manager: Teresa Graham
Director of Sales: Neil Levin
Director of Special Sales: Liz Ziehl
Director of New Product Development: Regina Hall
Managing Editor: Donia Ann Steele
Creative Director: Gary Stoiber
Production Manager: Carolyn Mills Bounds
Quality Assurance Manager: Miriam P. Newton
Picture Coordinator: Ruth Goldberg

Parts of this volume previously published in the series *This Fabulous Century.*

Series Editor: Ezra Bowen

Editorial Staff for *1940-1950: The Patriotic Tide*
Picture Editors: Mary Y. Steinbauer, Carlotta Kerwin
Designer: John R. Martinez
Assistant Designer: Jean Lindsay Morein
Staff Writers: Tony Chiu, Sam Halper, Anne Horan, Lucille Schulberg, Gerald Simons, Bryce S. Walker, Edmund White, Peter Yerkes
Researchers: Alice Baker, Terry Drucker, Marcia A. Gillespie, Helen Greenway, Lea Guyer, Helen M. Hinkle, Carol Isenberg, Nancy J. Jacobson, Myra Mangan, Mary Kay Moran, Patricia Smalley, Johanna Zacharias
Design Assistant: Anne B. Landry
Production Manager: Prudence G. Harris
Quality Assurance Manager: James King

CORRESPONDENTS: Elisabeth Kraemer-Singh (Bonn), Christine Hinze (London), Christina Lieberman (New York), Maria Vincenza Aloisi (Paris), Ann Natanson (Rome).

Valuable assistance was also provided by: Norman Airey, J. Patrick Barker, Jane Beatty, Pam Burke, Patricia Chandler, Murray J. Gart, Juliane Greenwalt, Blanche Hardin, Sandra Hindson, Dick Hitt, George Karas, Joan Gerard Larkin, Frank Leeming, Jr., Benjamin Lightman, Holland McCombs, Nancy McDonald, Frank Ney, Doris O'Neil, Richard Rawe, Jane Reiker, William Roberts, Gayle Rosenberg, George Thruston, Phyllis Wise, Sue Wymelenberg.

Editorial Staff for *1950-1960: Shadow of the Atom*
Picture Editor: Mary Y. Steinbauer
Designer: Charles Mikolaycak
Assistant Designer: Jean Lindsay Morein
Text Associate: Carlotta Kerwin
Staff Writers: Betsy Frankel, Sam Halper, Anne Horan, Lucille Schulberg, Gerald Simons, David Thompson, Bryce S. Walker, Edmund White, Peter Yerkes
Researchers: Alice Baker, Jill Beasley, Evelyn Constable, Terry Drucker, Marcia A. Gillespie, Helen Greenway, David Harrison, Helen M. Hinkle, Carol Isenberg, Nancy J. Jacobson, Myra Mangan, Mary Kay Moran, Patricia Smalley, Gabrielle Smith, Johanna Zacharias
Design Assistant: Anne B. Landry
Production Manager: Prudence G. Harris
Quality Assurance Manager: James King

CORRESPONDENTS: Elisabeth Kraemer-Singh (Bonn), Maria Cincenza Aloisi (Paris), Ann Natanson (Rome).

Valuable assistance was also provided by: Norman Airey, Jane Beatty, Pam Burke, Nicholas Costino, Jr. , Murray J. Gart, Juliane Greenwalt, George Karas, Joan Larkin, Frank Leeming, Jr., Benjamin Lightman, Holland McCombs, Doris O'Neil, Jane Reiker, Gayle Rosenberg, Phyllis Wise.

First printing. Printed in U.S.A.
Published simultaneously in Canada.

Library of Congress Cataloging-in-Publication Data

The good old days : America : the forties and the fifties / [the editors of Time-Life Books]
        p.   cm.
    Includes biographical references and index.
    ISBN 0-7835-4845-1
    1. United States--History--1945-1953--Miscellanea.   2. United States--History--1953-1961--Miscellanea.   3. United States--History--1933-1945--Miscellanea.
4. Popular culture--United States--History--Miscellanea.   I. Time-Life Books.
E813.G63 1996
973--dc20   96-8548
                                                                              CIP

Books produced by Time-Life Custom Publishing are available
at special bulk discount for promotional and premium use.
Custom adaptations can also be created to meet
your specific marketing goals. Call 1-800-323-5255.

CONTENTS

A Sentimental Journey

Sometimes one line from a song brings it all back. "I'll be seeing you in all the old familiar places ... " "Maybelline—why can't you be true?" "He's the boogie-woogie bugle boy of Company B. ... " Sometimes it's an image: black-browed Joseph McCarthy glowering across a microphone. Kilroy peering impudently over the nearest wall. And sometimes, to our dismay, the most vivid memories return with the bouncy chirp of a commercial jingle—the "Chiquita Banana Song," let's say. This volume, *The Good Old Days*, evokes the tunes, images, and events, both grand and trivial, that entered the consciousness of everyday Americans in the '40s and '50s.

These were decades rich in memorable moments, beginning explosively with the advent of World War II. Ripped away from the self-absorption of the depression, made to take a serious role in world affairs, Americans of the 1940s reacted to their new challenge with a surge of patriotic fervor. As millions of men went to war, millions of women took their places in offices and factories. Children searched garages for reusable rubber. Adults of all ages drank chicory coffee and learned to carpool. "When you ride ALONE," noted the poster, "you ride with Hitler!" In the face of grim news abroad, Americans thought positive—in fact, "Ac-cent-tchu-ate the Positive" was a popular wartime song, as were "When the Lights Go On Again (All over the World)" and the goofy "Mairzy Doats."

As the country moved from the single-minded sacrifices of the war years toward the prosperity of the '50s, its culture changed rapidly. The late '40s brought the flickering gray light of the television into American homes for the first time. The era of Frank Sinatra and Peggy Lee passed, not painlessly, into that of Buddy Holly and Chuck Berry. Broadway blossomed with classic musicals and dramas. Chevrolets packed with growing families rolled into the suburbs.

And yet this upbeat era was also marked by conflict and anxiety. Forced out of their isolationist stance by Pearl Harbor, Americans were shocked to find themselves vulnerable to aggression. Even when the war ended, it was with the ominous aid of an atomic bomb. "In some crude sense," said J. Robert Oppenheimer, developer of the bomb, "the physicists have known sin and this is a knowledge which they cannot lose." The same could be said of all Americans, who met the possibility of nuclear warfare with a mixture of dread, black humor, and half-hearted attempts at protection.

Hollywood camera crews filmed the construction of one of the first bomb shelters, in 1951, at the home of Mrs. Ruth Calhoun. "It will make a wonder-

6

ful place for the children to play in," she told reporters, "and it will be a good storehouse, too. I do a lot of canning and bottling in the summer, you know." B-movie monsters such as Godzilla and the "crawling eye" gave shape to nuclear anxieties—and were slain by the good guys at the end of the picture. By 1959 a graveyard humorist named Tom Lehrer evoked hollow chuckles with his song lyrics: "And we will all go together when we go, / Every Hottentot and every Eskimo; / When the air becomes uranious, / We will all go simultaneous, / Yes, we will all go together when we go."

Yet even in the shadow of the mushroom cloud, life went on. People settled down in front of TV sets to watch *Gunsmoke,* in which violence struck at a slower and more understandable pace. They took dance lessons and went to college in unprecedented numbers, and they applauded the adventurous spirit of a New Zealander named Edmund Hillary who climbed to the top of Mount Everest.

Internationally, the postwar years were marked by the restructuring of Europe and the beginning of the Cold War. Shaken by the doom so narrowly averted in World War II, American politicians reacted violently to the new menace of communism abroad and at home. In Fulton, Missouri, Winston Churchill put it eloquently. " A shadow has fallen upon the scenes so lately lighted by the Allied victory," he said. "From Stettin in the Baltic to Trieste in the Adriatic an iron curtain has descended across the Continent." Soon Americans went again to war, except this time it was in the unfamiliar territory of Korea, and the war was never called a war. An obscure Wisconsin senator named McCarthy rode to fame and eventual annihilation on the back of national concern about "Reds." In the process he became possibly the first— but not the last—politician ever destroyed by television. Gathering at homes and in theaters to watch the Army-McCarthy hearings, Americans finally came to agree with McCarthy's opponent, Joseph Welch, when he said "Have you no sense of decency, sir, at long last? Have you no sense of decency?"

In the home families grew and grew again. As the GIs returned, couples married in record numbers and split up at a record pace as well, with divorces soaring from 264,000 in 1940 to 610,000 in 1946. Women, pushed into employment during the war and dragged from it afterward, adjusted to a domestic existence. (Much to the disgust of novelist Fannie Hurst, who exclaimed, "A sleeping sickness is spreading among the women of the land ... they are retrogressing into ... that thing known as The Home.") As city dwellers moved into the suburbs, women turned their energies as volunteers into shoring up the wealth of new schools, libraries, and parks.

Without a war to focus their attention, teenagers began to act up and act out, much to the alarm of older observers. Teenage marriages increased dramatically, as did the birthrate among teens. Rates of juvenile delinquency began to rise by the end of the '40s, and not just among boys. In one example, teenage babysitters Roberta McCauley, Eileen Jeffreys, and Marilyn Curry, bored with their evening assignment, stole $18,000 from their employer's house and went on a shopping spree in New York City, buying Dior suits, dying their hair, and eventually picking up a prizefighter to take to a hotel. Questioned by the press the next day, Miss Jeffreys had this to say, "Don't say I've been smoking. My father would kill me if he knew."

And yet teenagers exerted a growing influence on the media of the day. With money in their pockets, teens spurred the growth of drive-in movies, fan magazines, and most memorably, rock and roll music. By 1958 teenagers were buying 70 percent of all albums produced. Although crooners such as Frank Sinatra had captured adolescent hearts in the war years, in the decade after the war teenagers began to crave something different, music that belonged to them, not their parents. The roots of rock and roll lay deep in African-American blues and jazz, as well as country music, but by the 1950s the new sound had been appropriated by mostly white, mainstream teenagers. Chuck Berry, Buddy Holly, the Shirelles, Little Richard, and the like cranked up the volume of the teenage experience. Most notorious of all, though, was probably that truckdriver from Memphis, Elvis Presley. Declared "an unspeakably untalented and vulgar entertainer" by the *New York Herald Tribune*, Elvis made it all too clear to worried parents that sexual energy and rock and roll were part of the same package.

Adolescent rebellion may have been inextricably connected to the country's new prosperity and status-quo attitude. After a burst of postwar inflation, Americans' standard of living reached a new high. Government assistance, union benefits, student loans, and housing subsidies greatly eased the economic inequality of the '30s and '40s. For the first time, white-collar workers began to outnumber manual laborers. By the 1950s the average wage earner could buy a median-priced home with a comfortable 15 to 18 percent of his income—and stock it with the new electric clothes dryers, disposals, and automatic dishwashers that were now on the market.

But a rising tide doesn't necessarily lift all ships. After long years of institutional discrimination, African-Americans were running out of patience.

People who had once again proved their courage and patriotism in the war were not interested in sitting in the back of anyone's bus. In the '40s, black athletes, led by Jackie Robinson, entered major league baseball. "Late, late as it was," wrote baseball commissioner Bart Giamatti later, "the arrival in the majors of Jack Roosevelt Robinson was an extraordinary moment in American history. For the first time, a black American was on America's most privileged version of a level field." In the '50s, Thurgood Marshall took on segregated education in the Supreme Court. Martin Luther King, Jr. led a boycott of Montgomery, Alabama, buses in 1956, despite threats to his life and the bombing of his home. There was a long road ahead, but as the '60s came into view, it was clear there was no going back.

Less visible than social protest, but no less influential in the course of future decades, were the scientific discoveries of the war and after. Advances in medicine included the discovery or manufacture of penicillin, sulfadiazine, quinine, cortisone, and oral contraceptives, and the introduction of vaccines for mumps, polio, and measles. The transatlantic team of Watson and Crick discovered the structure of DNA. The Soviet Union and the United States vied to launch satellites into space. And the first computers appeared, beginning with the huge, vacuum-tube-laden ENIAC, and mutating quickly to marketable transistor-based computers by 1959.

By themselves, the discovery of the genetic code and the invention of the transistor were profoundly important events; but like scientific advances in any age, they didn't make much of a dent on the awareness of the average U.S. citizen (although the transistor radio made a handy teenage accessory). Most people were busy with the here and now. They relaxed with their growing families in the comfort of their new homes, watching *Dragnet* and eating meaty home dinners. They joined their pals at the roller rink. Children wore Davy Crockett coonskin caps as they rode their two-wheelers down the sidewalk. Sports fans marveled or shuddered at the dominance of the New York Yankees (this was "when rooting for the Yankees was like rooting for U.S. Steel," as one commentator put it). Hula-Hoops, pogo sticks, 3-D glasses and chlorophyll gum kept folks amused. In short, life went on in the way that most of us now remember it. In the following pages is a fond trip through the mix of bobbysox and bombs, ration stamps and rock and roll that made up the central years of our century.

Teenagers

Bobbysoxers attain high fashion by mismatching shoes and socks.

Acne vs. the A-Bomb

Few young people share deeply in the life of a group dedicated, and actively devoted, to the highest goals of mankind. SOCIAL SCIENTIST MURRAY G. ROSS, 1950

I think you should have more articles on dates and shyness and put in some more about movie stars, too. Stories like those on atomic energy are very boring. LETTER TO THE EDITOR OF *SEVENTEEN* MAGAZINE, 1946

Once upon a time the awkward, gangling Americans living between grammar school and a job were deplored as creatures called adolescents. But by the mid-'40s, a notable change had occurred in the status of the adolescent. Suddenly, he emerged with the brand-new—and far more respectable—label of teenager. Adolescence evolved into a cult, to be prolonged, enjoyed, and commercially catered to as never before.

No one will ever know for sure how or why this change occurred. Clearly, though, the war played a major role. With everyone over 18 in the service, younger boys were often the biggest men in town. And for the first time since the Depression, they had money in their pockets, picked up in the many jobs available in the scarce labor market. Girls, too, earned spending money in a new profession: baby-sitting for parents on night shifts at war plants.

The teen-age phenomenon was quickly spotted—and boosted—by a variety of shrewd merchandisers. Among the first to cash in on the teen market were song writers and the manufacturers of phonographic equipment. In the strictly female market, Minx Modes, one of the healthiest members of a family of booming junior-fashions manufacturers, sold $12 million worth of frocks be-

tween 1944 and 1946. In the former year appeared *Seventeen,* a magazine solely devoted to the fashions, foibles and problems of young girls. Stadium Girl lipstick and other make-up blossomed on thousands of high-school faces; the Chicago *Daily News* started a wildly popular column of teen-age news titled Keen Teens; in 1949 the august *Ladies' Home Journal* inaugurated a new section called Profile of Youth; and all across the nation teen-age canteens became prime watering holes for jitterbugs and milk-shake drinkers on weekend evenings.

Throughout this early stage of the teen-age revolution, the kids themselves remained responsive to traditional parental discipline, became almost compulsively conformist within their own age group, and were massively unconcerned with world problems. A survey carried out by Purdue University to define the major concerns of teen-agers in the '40s revealed that 33 per cent felt there was nothing they, personally, could or should do to prevent wars; 50 per cent of all girls regarded their own figures as their No. 1 preoccupation; 37 per cent of all boys were primarily concerned with having "a good build"; and one third of all those 2,000 questioned agreed that the most serious problem facing the American teenager was acne.

Card sharks relax in the privacy of a buddy's place. Walls festooned with filched signs and Petty girls were de rigueur for teen-age boys' rooms.

The overwhelming urge of the teenager of the '40s was to be like every other teenager. Girls, especially, looked like peas in a disheveled pod—and the pod was often borrowed from the males. Though the girls never went so far as to wear the Army boots *(upper right)* affected by hordes of schoolboys, they did appear in baggy, rolled-up blue jeans and sloppy shirttails, and even striped football socks. On dates, however, the youngsters took care to be appropriately feminine. In pursuit of this goal the girls devoured all kinds of advice from magazines, newspapers and books *(excerpted below)* on how to do the Right Thing—i.e., hold the interest of the notoriously distractible young male.

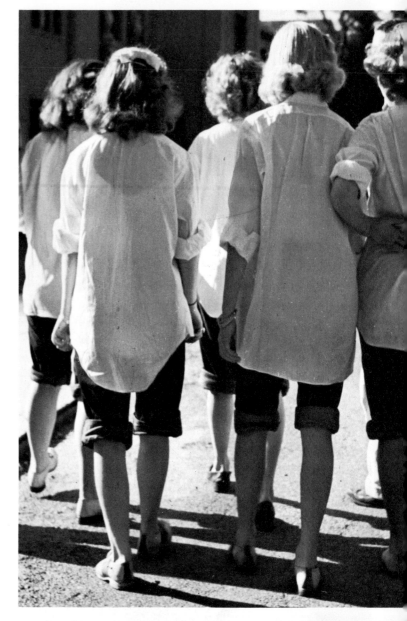

The moment with the family may be a bad one . . . but the next moment, when you are alone with Jimmy for the first time, may hold even greater terrors. What are you going to talk about? Bravely you start something: "Gee . . . it's hot tonight, isn't it?" Your voice trails—and dies. You've had your say. And one that requires nothing more than "Yes" or "No" from Jimmy. Which is no way to start a conversation. Jimmy may be just as shy as you are. His heart is thumping . . . his thoughts running round and round—just like yours. A smart Teen-Ager thinks about how to start a conversation with Jimmy long before she closes the front door behind her. This does not mean planned sentences —copying Susie's line, popping out with the newest slang phrase every other minute. It means figuring out subjects of mutual interest that make good conversation easy. Look over these conversation starters:

Tell Jimmy you remember the first time you ever laid eyes on him: "It was the first day of school three years ago in Latin class and you were wearing a red tie."

Talk about animals. "My dog has fleas—what'll I do?"

Talk about foreign languages: "Are you taking French?" "Have you ever traveled?" EDITH HEAL, *TEEN-AGE MANUAL*, 1948

Not Many Rebels

Though parents, as always, saw their teenagers as flagrant nonconformists, most kids lived and dressed (below) by rigid codes.

Regulation gear included sloppy trousers, loafers and dangling shirttails.

Preparing for a coed picnic, fraternity boys at a Kansas college toss blankets

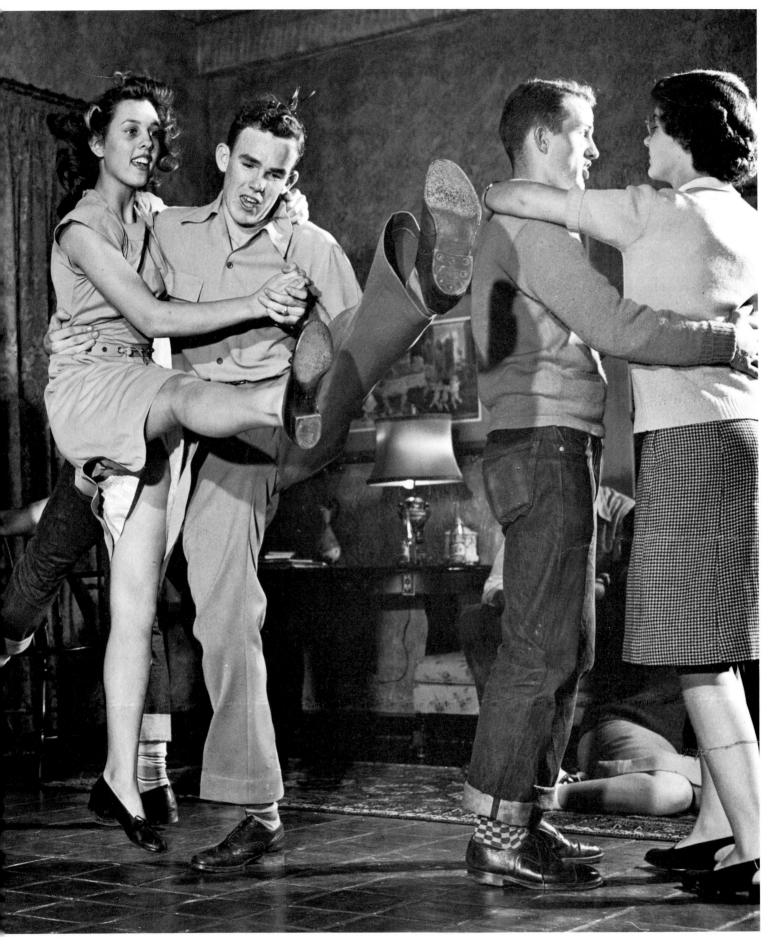

Partygoers in Porterville, California, do a fast lindy. To sell teenagers their records, RCA in 1950 gave away $10 in 45 rpm's with every $40 player.

The Idols of the Young

Seeking an insight into the values of modern youth, "Life" magazine in 1950 invited teenagers across the country to list the individual they admired most. The result was the dozen heroes below. Interpreting these choices, one college professor approved the idealizing of "muscle, brawn and brain," but found the admiration of "movie and radio people possibly a less reassuring trend."

TOP ROW: AUTHOR LOUISA MAY ALCOTT, BASEBALL PLAYER JOE DI MAGGIO AND SONG-AND-DANCE GIRL VERA-ELLEN. BOTTOM ROW: PRESIDENTS FRANKLIN D. ROOSEVELT AND ABRAHAM LINCOLN AND MOVIE COWPOKE ROY ROGERS.

TOP ROW: ARMY GENERAL DOUGLAS MACARTHUR, RED CROSS FOUNDER CLARA BARTON AND ACTRESS-SINGER DORIS DAY. BOTTOM ROW: SISTER ELIZABETH KENNY, BASEBALL HOME RUN HITTER BABE RUTH AND NURSE FLORENCE NIGHTINGALE.

Frank Sinatra aims a hungry gaze at the audience as he slides through a lyric. His sultry style earned him well over one million dollars per year.

The Voice

On the morning of October 12, 1944—Columbus Day in the third grim year of World War II—a frail-looking youth with rumpled brown hair stepped onto the stage of the Paramount Theater in New York City. Expectant squeals broke from the 3,600 teen-age girls who had packed the house. Then, as the youth started singing, his blue eyes searching hungrily among the faces in front of him, his voice tender and silky, the audience exploded. Adolescent voices screamed in genuine ecstasy at each slowly modulated musical phrase. Scores of schoolgirls swooned from their seats at each golden note, and ushers with smelling salts and stretchers hastened to revive them.

Outside, in Times Square, the commotion was even greater. Some 10,000 frenzied bobbysoxers had laid siege to the Paramount box office. Twenty thousand others clogged the square, blocking traffic, trampling bystanders and crashing through store windows. An emergency contingent of more than 700 riot police, including 200 patrolmen transferred from the Columbus Day Parade, was hastily called in to restore order.

The cause of all this ruckus was Francis Albert Sinatra, a crooner of romantic ballads whose voice reminded one critic of worn velveteen and another of the cry of a lovesick loon. Known variously as The King of Swoon, Frank Swoonatra, The Voice That Thrills Millions, or simply The Voice, he was a totally new phenomenon. No other entertainer, not even Rudy Vallee or good old Bing Crosby, had ever inspired such wild adulation, such total surrendering collapse. According to one listener, it was as though Frankie had musk glands instead of vocal cords.

Adults were mystified. "As a visible male object of adulation, Sinatra is baffling," *Newsweek* confessed. And at a time when the accepted image of American manliness was a brawny soldier in combat fatigues, Sinatra indeed seemed an unlikely idol. At five feet ten and 135 pounds, the young singer seemed on the verge of collapse from malnutrition; the big gag in show biz was that you could not tell which was Sinatra and which was the microphone. Frankie's clothes only accentuated his general scrawniness. For daytime performances he wore enormous, high-waisted slacks, flashy sport jackets with immense padded shoulders and outsized bow ties that flopped like spaniels' ears. Said trumpeter Harry James, one of his early employers, "He looks like a wet rag."

Even Frankie's singing failed to convince some skeptics. "The swooner-crooner who makes every song sound just like every other song," sneered LIFE, could render in only one lugubrious tempo: "largo alla marcia funebre." Another critic complained that listening to Sinatra was like "being stroked by a hand covered with cold cream." But most of his fellow musicians were as enthusiastic as the bobbysoxers. "Call it talent," said torch singer Jo Stafford. "You knew he couldn't do a number badly."

Obviously it was more than Sinatra's well-tuned ear and evocative phrasing that galvanized the bobbysoxers. "Personally, I think it's on account of his personality," one young lady declared flatly. Various psychiatrists analyzed it differently: "mass hypnotism," "mass frustrated love," "mammary hyperesthesia," and, referring to Sinatra's wispy build, a maternal "urge to feed the hungry." Several commentators pointed out, with a modicum of cruel accuracy, that, with most young men in the army, Frankie was the only male around.

Sinatra himself had a simple explanation. "I'm twenty-five. I look maybe nineteen," he said. "Most of the kids feel like I'm one of them—the pal next door, say. So maybe they feel they know me. And that's the way I want it to be. What the hell, they're nice kids." And Sinatra did in fact seem to be a teenager himself—so vulnerable, so shy, so sincere, so terribly innocent.

But The Voice That Thrills Millions was, in reality, about as frail and innocent as an Army Ranger. He was born on December 12, 1915, in a cold-water tenement in the rugged waterfront section of Hoboken, New Jersey. From his father, a Sicilian immigrant who at one time made his way as a bantamweight prizefighter, Sinatra gained a taste for bare-knuckle brawling. From his strong-minded mother, who was active in local politics, he inherited a king-sized ambition and a quicksilver temper. By the time he had dropped out of high school, in the middle of his sophomore year, the skinny Sinatra had fought his way to leadership of a local gang of toughs. Crafty and cocky, he was dubbed "Angles" by his friends.

In 1933, at age 17, Frankie hit upon the Big Angle. He happened to buy tickets to a Bing Crosby concert at a local movie house, and became utterly entranced, both by Crosby's voice and his power over the public. "I can do that!" he exclaimed to his date, childhood sweetheart Nancy Barbato. Nancy, who loved him so much that she eventually married him, agreed.

The next seven years were a rough uphill battle for recognition. He sang at lodge meetings, entered amateur contests, filled in at local radio stations (his fee was 70 cents for carfare). In 1939, while he was singing at a small Jersey roadhouse, he was discovered and signed by Harry James, who was just starting his own band. Six months later, Frankie moved up to a spot with Tommy Dorsey, who was then one of the nation's top bandleaders. Over

---

I can sing that son of a bitch off the stage any day of the week.
SINATRA ON ANY RIVAL, 1945

---

the next two years with Dorsey, he was a screaming success in club dates, cut a basketful of hit records including "Fools Rush In," "White Christmas" and "Night and Day," and was on his way to becoming a national celebrity.

In the winter of 1942, Sinatra set out on his own. He bought out his contract with Dorsey, hired a press agent, and on December 30, 1942, opened the first of his notoriously successful engagements at the Paramount. A girl in the audience (who reportedly had not eaten lunch) swooned during the performance. Another girl squealed, and bedlam ensued. From then on, he was The Voice.

The epidemic of Sinatritis swept like measles through the nation's teenagers. Two thousand fan clubs sprang up, and the singer's fan mail rose to 5,000 letters a week. To get an autograph, frantic bobbysoxers would lie in wait in Frankie's dressing room or pursue him to nightclubs, restaurants and even to his home, where they would peek through the windows and try to climb into his bedroom. When it snowed, some of them lovingly dug up his

footprints and preserved them in the refrigerator. Others tried to tear off Frankie's clothes, and twice the singer barely escaped strangulation when two girls staged a frenetic tug of war with his bow tie. Even a few older women succumbed; one adult admirer approached him in the Waldorf hotel in 1943, ripped open her bodice and demanded he autograph her bra.

Frankie thrived on such hazards of success. "I'm riding high, kid," he told one reporter. And indeed he was. Within months of his Paramount debut, The Voice had hooked into a gilt-edged contract with Columbia Records to turn out his songs, signed to appear each week on *Your Hit Parade* and contracted with RKO to make a movie a year. His income leaped to a million dollars annually, and he moved to Hollywood, where he built a pink house that had a $7,000 machine just to close the curtains on one wall. Always impulsively generous with friends, he began passing out $150 gold cigarette lighters as though they were Baby Ruths.

Meanwhile the reaction of American adults ranged from mystification to outrage. "We can't tolerate young people making a public display of losing control of their emotions," proclaimed a New York City education commissioner, George Chatfield. The commissioner then threatened to press charges against Sinatra for encouraging truancy since thousands of girls were skipping school to hear him sing. In Congress, according to the *New York Herald Tribune*, it was stoutly affirmed that "The Lone Ranger and Frank Sinatra are the prime instigators of juvenile delinquency in America." In Hollywood the formidable columnist Elsa Maxwell charged the singer with "musical illiteracy" and further recommended that Frankie's fans be given "Sinatraceptives."

Much of the adult dislike of Frank Sinatra stemmed from an odd sort of affronted patriotism. Somehow it seemed unfair, while thousands of brave American lads were giving their lives on foreign beachheads, for a pint-sized entertainer back home to be earning millions of dollars as well as the adoration of the country's teen-age girls. "Is there no way to make those kids come to their senses?" asked a refugee from a German concentration camp, herself 17 years old. "The time they are wasting outside the Paramount Theater could be used for other purposes—for instance, to help win this war."

And it was true that Sinatra himself made little contribution to the war effort, though the failure to do so was not altogether his fault. He was called up on several occasions to take an Army physical exam—while tearful bobbysoxers mobbed the induction center—but he was classified 4-F because of a punctured eardrum. He did make one USO tour of Italy in 1945, shortly after V-E Day. And on returning home, he evoked the wrath of both soldiers and civilians by charging that the USO program was run by "shoemakers in uniform." "Mice make women faint, too," snidely observed the Army newspaper *Stars and Stripes*, and Marlene Dietrich, who had sung to frontline troops while enemy shells were bursting overhead, remarked that "you could hardly expect the European Theater to be like the Paramount."

Adult distaste for Frankie hung on past V-J Day. Ironically, it assaulted him even when he did something courageous and right. Sinatra had always possessed an instinctive urge to do battle for the underdog and had once impulsively slugged a counterman at a restaurant for refusing to serve blacks. In 1945 he launched his own national campaign to stamp out racial prejudice. He preached tolerance on radio shows, to theater audiences and in high school auditoriums across the country. In 1946 he won a special Academy Award for a movie short on racial intolerance called *The House I Live In*.

Many Sinatraphobes had a hard time taking Frankie's crusading seriously. Others took outright offense. His tolerance campaign drew a barrage of fire from various right-wingers. The conservative Hearst newspaper chain hinted that Frankie was a Communist and in 1947 ran unsubstantiated stories that he was up for investigation by the House Committee on Un-American Activities.

Most of the hate-Sinatra barrage was similar, irresponsible hip-shooting. But something close to a bull's-eye came in February 1947 from Scripps-Howard columnist Robert Ruark, who at the time was following up a lead on the recently exiled Mafia boss, "Lucky" Luciano. Ruark had tracked Luciano to earth in Havana, where he found the racket czar surrounded by henchmen and apparently carrying on business much as usual. But whom should Ruark spot among the goons and bodyguards, consorting with America's most sinister crook, but—horror of horrors—Frank Sinatra, America's teen dream! "This curious desire to cavort among the scum is possibly permissible

---

Nobody comes before my wife Nancy. That goes for now and for all time. SINATRA ON MATRIMONY, 1943

among citizens who are not peddling sermons to the nation's youth," admonished Ruark. "But Mr. Sinatra, the self-confessed savior of the country's small fry, seems to be setting a most peculiar example to his hordes of pimply, shrieking slaves."

The Voice fought back, verbally at first. "Any report that I fraternized with goons or racketeers is a vicious lie," he protested. But Frankie's gut response to such criticism was to use his fists. In April, while dining with friends at a fancy Hollywood restaurant, Sinatra spotted one of his loudest detractors, New York *Daily Mirror* writer Lee Mortimer, in a nearby booth. The way Mortimer told it, he got up to leave when suddenly he was jumped from behind by Sinatra and three thugs. The attack, said Mortimer, was a totally unprovoked surprise.

Frankie's version was notably different. "He gave me a look," the singer said. "He called me a dago son of a bitch, and I saw red." No one really knows who said what, but Sinatra ended up by paying Mortimer $9,000 in damages, admitting, "We all have our human weaknesses."

Other flaws began to show in the bobbysoxers' idol. For years Frankie had been billed as Hollywood's ideal husband. Now, showing a distinct taste for high-priced cheesecake, he deserted his wife Nancy and his three children. After a round of purported infidelities with various starlets, in February 1950 the singer was spotted dining tête-à-tête with Ava Gardner, then Hollywood's reigning

femme fatale. When a news photographer tried to film the couple, Sinatra threatened to break his nose.

There followed a tumultuous public courtship. With the press gleefully dogging his heels, the thoroughly smitten Frankie chased Ava back to Hollywood, to New York, to Spain (where the actress made a movie, and had an extracurricular fling with a bullfighter) and home again. The newspapers published each spicy detail: where the couple shared hotel rooms, where they did not; whether Frank gave Ava a $10,000 emerald necklace ("The only present I ever gave Ava was six bottles of coke," Frank sourly grunted) or whether he did not; whether Sinatra would divorce his wife or whether Nancy would divorce him.

Through it all, a hostile press reported Sinatra's ever more violent temper fits and moods of deep depression. Not only was Frankie making a stupendous spectacle of himself, the impulsive brawler was falling apart under the impact of Ava, who was dubbed the "Avalanche" and who had already left two husbands shattered and wan.

Sinatra's life was disintegrating in other sectors as well. A movie he made during 1948, *Miracle of the Bells,* clanged hollowly at the box office. Sales of his records were slipping alarmingly, and in 1949 he was dropped from his spot on *Your Hit Parade.* Teen-age swooners began drifting away in disillusioned armies to listen to Frankie Laine, Perry Como and Billy Eckstine. To cap it off, Sinatra's silken vocal cords were beginning to fray from overuse. At a nightclub engagement in New York in 1950, he suffered a massive throat hemorrhage. It seemed The Voice was silenced for good.

"Is the frenzied, swooning bobby-soxer disappearing from the U.S. scene?" the New York *Star* had asked as early as 1948. Even Frankie had to admit that the party seemed to be over. "From what I can determine there's a definite trend among the bobby-soxers. They're growing up," he said. His voice gone, his fans departed, it seemed Sinatra was finished. Perhaps there would be another road back to the top for the welterweight scrapper from Hoboken. But at the decade's end, there was every sign that Frankie, himself, might be going into his last swoon.

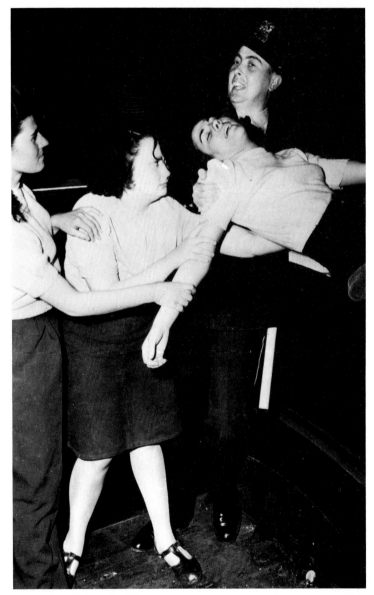

Wherever Frankie appeared, he was greeted by the wild adoration of what one critic called "imbecilic, moronic, screaming-meemie autograph kids."

Marines swarm over a Japanese bunker on Tarawa.

The Day the Cat Jumped

Everything was ready. From Rangoon to Honolulu every man was at battle stations.
TIME MAGAZINE, LAST ISSUE BEFORE PEARL HARBOR

I don't know how the hell we were caught so unprepared.
JOE MARTIN, HOUSE REPUBLICAN LEADER, DECEMBER 8, 1941

Never in American history was an event more anticipated yet more of a surprise than the attack on Pearl Harbor. The tactics of a sneak raid on Pearl—crippling the formidable U.S. fleet based there and freeing the Japanese Navy to dominate the Pacific—had been a standard part of both Tokyo's and Washington's strategic thinking for a decade. From 1931 on, every graduating class at Japan's naval academy had faced the same final exam question: "How would you carry out a surprise attack on Pearl Harbor?" In 1932 a U.S. carrier showed how: sneaking in northeast of the island of Oahu in a pre-dawn "raid," its planes "sank" all the vessels at Pearl. Japanese observers reported the feat; Tokyo carefully recorded it.

In mid-1941, the theoretical danger to Pearl became very real. The long-standing rivalry between Japan and the U.S. for Pacific supremacy, bitterly sharpened by Japan's rape of China, was further aggravated by announced plans for broad expansion of Nippon's Greater East Asia Co-Prosperity Sphere. In effect this meant that all white devils were going to be kicked out of Asia. To check the Japanese momentum, the U.S. had already embargoed American oil and scrap metals—both vital to Japan's war machine. Then, in July, President Roosevelt brought mat-

ters to a head by freezing all Japanese assets in the U.S.

At the Imperial Palace in Tokyo, the militarists said there was now no alternative but war—and soon. Strike, they argued, before the U.S. embargo so weakened Japan and Roosevelt's push toward rearmament so strengthened the U.S. that the moment would be lost. With Emperor Hirohito's cautious help Japan's peacefully inclined civilian leaders won a compromise: the diplomats would get until November 29 to try for an accommodation with Washington; failing that, war.

A race began: talks in Washington, war preparations in Japan. In Washington, Japan's prime peace-talker was bumbling, kindly, 62-year-old Ambassador Kichisaburo Nomura. Given to hearty belly laughs and good whiskey, Nomura was an old Potomac hand; as naval attaché in Washington during World War I, he had worked with Assistant Secretary of the Navy Franklin D. Roosevelt. F.D.R. now welcomed "my old personal friend" to the White House for nine separate, chummy talks; and Tokyo's civilian chiefs allowed themselves a flicker of hope. To join the talks later came Special Envoy Saburo Kurusu, no old Presidential pal but a smooth diplomat with an American wife. Almost daily Nomura chattered away

Envoys Kurusu (left) and Nomura leave the State Department after a peace conference with Secretary Hull just 17 days before Pearl Harbor.

in his mournful singsong and heavy accent to U.S. Secretary of State Cordell Hull, who answered "that old codger" in a Tennessee drawl aggravated by ill-fitting dentures, so that neither fully understood the other.

Meanwhile, 13,000 miles away, 43 assorted admirals and captains in Japan's Navy War College schemed out the fleet plan for air attack on Pearl Harbor and decided it was feasible. Now, with Emperor Hirohito looking on anxiously, an elite group of hawks and doves secretly argued Japan's decision between peace and war.

The Emperor was not the only one watching. By a stroke of fortune so great that it was code-named "Magic," another small group of leaders—American leaders—were privy to Japan's agonized appraisal. Late in 1940 the Signal Corps had cracked "Purple," Japan's top diplomatic code, and after January 23, 1941, nine high U.S. government officials called "Ultras," among them President Roosevelt, were able every day to read the most secret communications between Tokyo and its diplomats.

"Magic" showed the Japanese doves growing increasingly downhearted about the negotiations. On October 16, Japan's civilian Premier, having barely escaped assassination by war hawks the month before and fearful that the next attempt would succeed, resigned with his cabinet; and General Hideki Tojo, a fire-eater, took over as Premier. Now the military was in the saddle. In Washington, the fascinated "Ultras"—via "Magic"—watched the danger draw closer and closer. November 4, 1941, Tokyo to Ambassador Nomura: "Relations between Japan and the U.S. have reached the edge. This is our last effort." November 22: "We will wait until Nov. 29. After that things are automatically going to happen."

But peace had already lost the race. On November 26, six radio-silenced Japanese carriers stole out of the remote Kuriles north of Japan, headed toward Pearl along the untraveled northern route. As the quiet, 32-ship fleet steamed in two parallel columns, another message flashed from Tokyo to Washington, November 28: "In two or three days negotiations will be de facto ruptured." Should Nomura yet perform a miracle in Washington, the attack

force could be recalled up to December 5. Else, the radio signal "Climb Mt. Niitaka" would send 353 carrier planes at dawn December 7 to blast the fleet at Pearl.

Pearl was in peril, but then almost every American war chief was supposed to have known it. On January 24, 1940, Navy Secretary Frank Knox wrote to Secretary of War Henry Stimson, "Hostilities would be initiated by a surprise attack on Pearl Harbor." In April 1941, joint estimates by the commanders of the Army and Navy air forces defending Pearl concluded that Japan "can probably employ a maximum of six carriers which would probably approach inside of 300 miles. A dawn air attack might be a complete surprise." The Pacific Fleet commander himself, Rear Admiral Husband E. Kimmel, had told his staff: "Declaration of war might be preceded by a surprise attack on Pearl Harbor."

"Magic," of course, continued to sound the signal of increasing danger. September 24, Tokyo to its Honolulu consulate general: "With regard to warships and aircraft carriers, report on those at anchor, tied up at wharves, buoys and in docks." November 29: "Report even when there are no [ship] movements."

That same day, Chief of Naval Operations Admiral Harold "Betty" Stark notified his Hawaii, Philippine and Panama commanders from Washington: "This is a war warning. An aggressive move by Japan is expected within the next few days." Indeed from Tokyo, December 3, came a further indication—"In view of present situation, let me know day by day if there are any observation balloons above Pearl Harbor"—and on December 5 the FBI in Hawaii warned Pearl that the Japanese consulate was burning its confidential papers. The next evening, December 6, F.D.R. soberly read the intercept of the first 13 parts of a climactic Tokyo message to envoys Nomura and Kurusu, breaking off negotiations forthwith. Said F.D.R. to Harry Hopkins: "This means war."

In the heaving, trackless North Pacific the silent striking force received the go signal: "Climb Mt. Niitaka." By 8 a.m. December 7 (2:30 a.m. in Hawaii) the men assigned to monitoring "Magic" in Washington decoded the 14th

The oily, black smoke of war rises from the wreckage of the Naval Air Station at Pearl Harbor. The Japanese attackers lost fewer than 100 men.

and final part of Japan's message to its emissaries: "It is impossible to reach an agreement. Submit to the U.S. government our reply at 1 p.m. on the seventh, your time."

War within the next few hours—but where? An Army colonel and a Navy commander involved in "Magic" both remarked that 1 p.m. in Washington was just after dawn at Pearl, the quiet time when crews were piped to breakfast. Panama and other possible danger spots had gone on full alert after the November 27 warning: airfields blacked out, radars in continuous operation, fighter planes and antiaircraft guns in readiness.

But at the prime objective—the home base of the fleet that was the greatest single deterrent to Japanese aggression and therefore the most logical point of attack—the Army, which was responsible for defending the base, put itself on the mildest of its three alerts, the No. 1 or anti-sabotage alert. This order parked the planes in bunches, the easier to guard them against sabotage (and the easier to bomb them). Antiaircraft guns were retained in parks, and ammunition in magazines, so that getting the guns into action would take one to four hours. Hawaii's five mobile radars operated not 24 hours daily but from 4 a.m. to 11 a.m. weekdays and from 4 a.m. to 7 a.m. weekends —weekends being days of rest at Pearl as in civilian U.S.

The Navy at Pearl also put itself on its loosest alert —Condition Three, meaning that but 25 per cent of its antiaircraft guns were manned. There were no barrage balloons, no torpedo nets, no reconnaissance planes. Virtually all fleet units were brought into Pearl and conveniently moored side by side. One third to one half the ships' officers were ashore.

Still, there was a little time to get set—and a host of 11th-hour warnings. At 6:45 a.m. December 7, the destroyer *Ward* radioed that it had ferreted out a Japanese midget sub and sunk it, firing what turned out to be the first American shot in the Pacific war. At 7:02 two soldiers, voluntarily staying overtime to train on one of the Army's five radar screens, reported seeing blips. None of these warnings was taken up. "Hell," said one officer of the radar blips, "it's probably just a pigeon with a metal band around its leg." The attackers were 50 minutes away.

"Pearl Harbor was still asleep in the morning mist," the commander of the lead Japanese formation recalled later. At 7:55 as the first of three attacking waves began its run, of 96 vessels at Pearl, one lone destroyer was under way. With the first bombs, hoarse klaxons calling General Quarters on every vessel shattered the Sabbath quiet and sounded the end of peace for the next 1,364 days. In 110 minutes eight big battleships and three light cruisers were sunk or damaged, 188 planes destroyed and 2,400 men killed. The Japanese accomplished this at a cost of 29 aircraft, five midget submarines and one fleet sub. They had expected to lose one third of the attack fleet. They lost none; their fleet was not even detected.

The blow not only paralyzed U.S. power in the Pacific for the greater part of a crucial year, it also laid bare America's inexcusable optimism and its unbelievable unreadiness for battle. The U.S. had had every possible warning. Yet when attack came, hardly an American failed to express stunned surprise. In Washington, as he received the first word of the raid, Navy Secretary Knox, who had warned of just such an attack the year before, blurted: "My God! This can't be true. This must mean the Philippines." "No sir," said Admiral Stark. "This is Pearl."

Before decade's end, six investigations would try to clarify what had happened and why. But despite 40 volumes of testimony, the whole affair would remain essentially a mystery. And the question would stick forever in the American craw: How could Pearl Harbor have happened?

Before America got ready for what lay ahead those next four years, there would be other bloody illustrations of the military's aptitude for what soon became known as the snafu (translated, bowdlerized, as Situation Normal, All Fouled Up). Just 10 hours after Pearl, with the Americans now fully alerted, there was a second surprise attack of almost equal magnitude. Japanese planes sweeping in from the north caught General Douglas MacArthur with his planes down and in some 80 minutes destroyed half the U.S. air arm in the Philippines. The Japanese lost seven fighters. The United States lost its innocence.

Where Were You When the Bombs Fell?

At 2:20 p.m. Washington time, 55 minutes after the attack started, White House Press Secretary Steve Early, at home in pajamas, got the press services simultaneously on the phone and released the news. That instant, like the snap of a camera's shutter, froze the American scene:

A commander on the bridge of the U.S.S. *Ramapo* banged away at the planes with a pistol. Tears laced his cheeks. A bosun's mate threw wrenches at the low-flying aircraft. From the magazine came a call asking what he needed. *"Powder,"* he yelled. *"I can't keep throwing things at them."*

Seaman Joseph Hydruska, 22, boarded the U.S.S. *Oklahoma,* which had taken six torpedoes below the waterline and was about to capsize. *"I was terribly afraid. We were cutting through with acetylene torches. First we found six naked men waist deep in water. They didn't know how long they had been down there and they were crying and moaning with pain. Some of them were very badly wounded. We could hear tapping all over the ship, SOS taps, no voices, just those eerie taps from all over. There was nothing we could do for most of them."*

A sergeant in the 27th Infantry at Pearl refused to issue ammunition. He pointed to a sign that said no ammunition without captain's orders.

The explosions awoke *Christian Science Monitor* correspondent Joseph Harsch in a Honolulu hotel. He thought how much it sounded like the air raids in Berlin, where he had been last year, and woke his wife: *"Darling, you've often asked what an air raid sounds like. Listen to this—it's a good imitation." "Oh, so that's what it's like,"* she said. They both dozed off again.

On the U.S.S. *San Francisco* a young engineer came topside and said to an ensign: *"Thought I'd come up and die with you."*

The gunners on the U.S.S. *Argonne* shot down their own antenna.

Battery B on Oahu was issued machine-gun ammunition dated 1918—so old the belts fell apart in the loading machines.

Near the married men's quarters at Pearl a gang of children jumped up and down screaming, *"Here come the Indians."*

Seaman "Squash" Marshall raced for cover from strafers at Kaneohe air station. As bullets snapped at his heels he actually seemed to outrun a Zero for 100 yards, then zagged to one side while the bullets pinged ahead. The men watching set up a great cheer as though he had made a touchdown.

Water swirled into the U.S.S. *California,* where Machinist's Mate Robert Scott in the forward air compressor station was trying to feed air to the 5-inch guns. The others ran, yelling to Scott to get out in a hurry. He shouted: *"This is my station—I'll stay here and give them air as long as the guns are going."* They let him have his way and shut the watertight door.

Dashing to get a better look at the bombing, a Honolulu man yelled at a reporter: *"The mainland papers will exaggerate this."*

An hour after an appeal for blood, 500 volunteers swamped Dr. John Devereux and three assistants at the Honolulu blood bank; they ran out of containers and used sterilized Coke bottles. Devereux's best volunteer, cleaning bottles and tubes, was a local prostitute.

Admiral Kimmel's orderly came out of the admiral's office at Pearl and said: *"He's tearing his hair out, saying 'What should I do, what should I do?'"*

In Pearl a wounded ensign begged a friend, *"Kill me."*

On the U.S.S. *New Orleans* at Pearl, Chaplain Howell Forgy told the gun crews he was sorry they didn't have church that morning but to *"praise the Lord and pass the ammunition."*

General Jonathan Wainwright in the Philippines jiggled the phone to get his aide. *"Johnny!" "Hello. . . . Yes, General." "The cat has jumped."*

Winston Churchill placed a phone call. *"Mr. President, what's this about Japan?" "It's quite true,"* said F.D.R. *"We're all in the same boat." "This actually simplifies things,"* said Churchill. *"God be with you."* He went to bed and slept soundly.

People in Phoenix phoned *The Arizona Republic* newsroom and asked: *"Have you got any score on the game between the Chicago Bears and the Cardinals? Aren't you getting anything besides that war stuff?"*

Ernest Vogt and his family continued eating their Sunday roast chicken dinner in New York City. *"I thought it was another Orson Welles hoax."*

A pretty, black-haired girl complained in Palm Springs: *"Everybody knew this was going to happen, so why spoil a perfectly good Sunday afternoon worrying about it?"*

In Pittsburgh, where Senator Gerald Nye had gone to address 2,500 hysterically isolationist America Firsters, a newsman told him of the attack on Pearl. Nye snapped: *"Sounds terribly fishy to me."*

At nightfall a sentry at Schofield Barracks near Pearl challenged three times, got no answer and shot one of his own mules.

Edward R. Murrow had been invited to dinner with the President that evening. His wife phoned the White House: were they still expected? Eleanor Roosevelt said: *"We all have to eat. Come anyway."* Later that night the President pounded the study table as he described to Murrow how the U.S. planes were destroyed *"on the ground, by God, on the ground."*

Ensign John F. Kennedy, U.S.N.R., was at Griffith Stadium in Washington watching the Redskins win, 20-14, over the Philadelphia Eagles. The Stadium did not give the news over the loudspeaker. Young Kennedy heard it over the car radio going home and immediately put in for active sea duty.

At a newsstand at Michigan and Randolph in Chicago, a fat woman saw the headlines and said: *"What's this?" "We're at war lady, for crying out loud." "Well, what do you know,"* she said. *"Who with?"*

F.D.R. called secretary Grace Tully into his study and started dictating: *"Yesterday comma December seven comma nineteen forty-one dash a date which will live in infamy dash."*

At Fort Sam Houston, a brigadier general catching up on sleep after weeks of tough field maneuvers got a phone call and his wife heard him say: *"Yes? When? I'll be right down."* As he rushed off, Dwight Eisenhower told Mamie he was going to headquarters and didn't know when he would be back.

A GI under enemy shellfire huddles in a ditch on Okinawa.

That artillery did things to you. We'd been
told not to duck when we heard the screaming of shells;
it would be too late. But we ducked anyway.
Even the almost silent pop of the mortars was frightening.
We got to know exactly where a shell would land.

A CORPORAL QUOTED IN THE GI NEWSPAPER *YANK*

Protected by naval gunfire, GIs invade Makin Island.

The Sea War

Although the Japanese bombing of Pearl Harbor destroyed or crippled 18 naval ships, including eight battleships, the disaster of December 7 pointed the way toward eventual U.S. victory. For even the most myopic old-line admiral could recognize in Pearl Harbor the power of carrier-based aircraft. From that time forward, carriers replaced battleships as the U.S. Navy's chief offensive weapon, thus revolutionizing warfare at sea.

The pattern for this new brand of sea war was set just six months after Pearl, in a weird, sprawling struggle in which, one Navy man wrote, "Nine tenths of the men engaged never saw the prize for which they fought." That prize was American-held Midway Island, which a Japanese armada was attempting to seize. The battle for Midway began on June 3, 1942, when the two fleets were 400 miles apart. For three days, great flights of bombers attacked each other's seagoing bases. On June 6, when the fleets finally disengaged, 403 planes had been shot down, 253 of them Japanese. Even more significant, the U.S. fleet had sunk four enemy carriers and lost only one, and Midway was safe. The reduction of Japan's navy was far from complete, but Admiral Chester Nimitz had grounds for making a jubilant pun: "We are about midway to that objective."

A sailor paints a fresh kill on a carrier scoreboard.

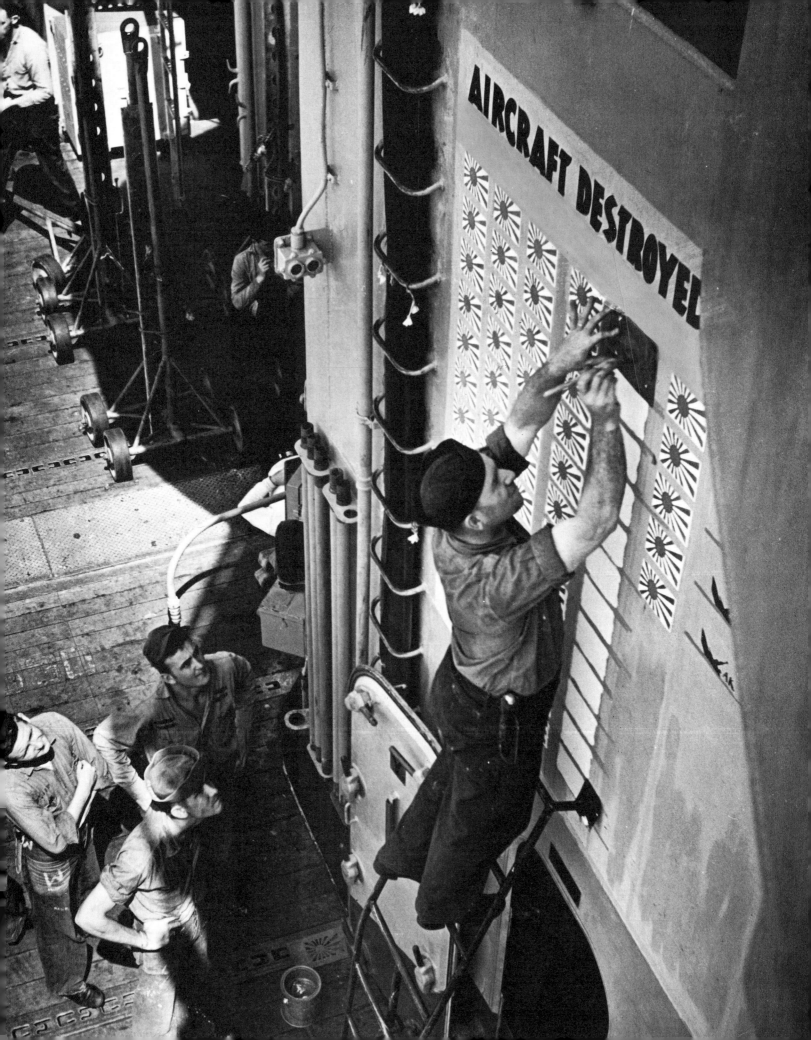

The Air War

Until the final year of the war, the only direct attack the English and Americans could mount upon Germany was through the air; and to do even that proved difficult, costly and harrowing. Hundreds of American planes were lost in the Atlantic crossing as freighters were sunk by German U-boats. Of the planes that reached Europe, 18,500 bombers and fighters—and 64,000 airmen—were shot down by Luftwaffe fighters and German antiaircraft batteries. The lives of the pilots and crewmen were one long series of contrasts: periods of easy routine on countryside bases, then the hours of tension on the missions. Many men cracked under the strain.

The air war reached its fierce crescendo early in 1944. Fed by the booming output of U.S. factories, the big fleets of Flying Fortress and Liberator bombers swelled into 1,000-plane armadas, and their losses were sharply reduced by convoys of long-range American fighter planes. Within a few months, these vast fighter-bomber flights had not only pounded German war plants and dozens of cities, but had virtually obliterated the Luftwaffe. Fortress Europe now lay vulnerable to attack by sea, and General Eisenhower could promise his invasion forces, "If you see fighting aircraft over you, they will be ours."

A weary crewman grabs a bite at an English base.

The Land War

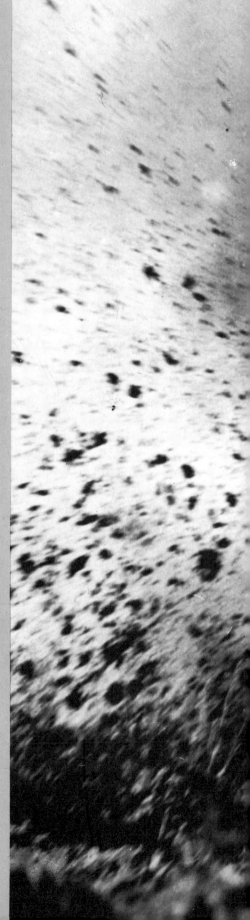

The basic premise of Allied grand strategy was that Germany could not finally be defeated until her land armies were destroyed. To put troops on the continent, the Western allies first invaded North Africa, in November 1942; within a year they had leapfrogged to Sicily and thence to southern Italy. Meanwhile even greater forces were being marshaled at English bases for a cross-Channel invasion. By May 1944, Britain was jammed with 2,876,000 troops—most of them American—and with millions of tons of supplies and equipment.

The materiel for the invasion was enormously sophisticated —multiple rocket-launchers, amphibious tanks, huge floating docks. Yet the basic unit for this modern assault was an old stand-by: the ordinary foot soldier, simply equipped with a rifle and ammunition, carrying the few other things he needed to survive, relying heavily on personal courage and resourcefulness. The rifleman alone could take enemy positions inaccessible to tanks and irreducible by air attack; and the primary purpose of the whole prodigious invasion build-up was to put 176,000 such troops onto German-held beaches on the first day of direct combat. When D-Day finally dawned on the historic morning of June 6, 1944, it was really I-Day—infantryman's day.

Beneath a shellburst, a paratrooper attacks in Holland.

Ike offers a last word to paratroopers before the D-Day takeoff.

A Touch of Ike

*On June 5, 1944, General Dwight D. Eisenhower
sent a message (below) to the vast Allied expeditionary force,
urging all to victory in the invasion of France
on the next day. Ike also scribbled a draft (bottom), never sent,
assuming personal responsibility in case of failure.*

You are about to embark upon the Great Crusade, toward which we have striven these many months. The eyes of the world are upon you. The hopes and prayers of liberty-loving people everywhere march with you. In company with our brave Allies and brothers-in-arms on other Fronts, you will bring about the destruction of the German war machine, the elimination of Nazi tyranny over the oppressed peoples of Europe, and security for ourselves in a free world.

Your task will not be an easy one. Your enemy is well trained, well equipped and battle-hardened. He will fight savagely.

But this is the year 1944! . . . The tide has turned! The free men of the world are marching together to Victory!

I have full confidence in your courage, devotion to duty and skill in battle. We will accept nothing less than full Victory!

Good Luck! And let us all beseech the blessing of Almighty God upon this great and noble undertaking.

Our landings in the Cherbourg-Havre area have failed to gain a satisfactory foothold and I have withdrawn the troops. My decision to attack at this time and place was based upon the best information available. The troops, the air and the Navy did all that bravery and devotion to duty could do. If any blame or fault attaches to the attempt it is mine alone.

First Lieutenant Audie Murphy obligingly displays two of his medals: the coveted Congressional Medal of Honor (left) and the Legion of Merit.

The Mostest Hero

Farmersville, Texas—population 2,206—turned out en masse on June 15, 1945, to welcome home Lieutenant Audie Murphy, recently returned from the battlefields of North Africa, Italy and France. A basically modest man, he listened with embarrassment as one dignitary after another lauded his combat record and dramatically recounted the heroic feat that won him the Congressional Medal of Honor with the citation quoted below. Yet the Farmersville reception touched Audie deeply. The mayor's speech was matched in generosity by the gifts of the townspeople, who remembered Audie's hard times as the orphaned boy of sharecroppers. Murphy had a tear in his eye as he thanked his friends and then sent them home: "I know you people don't want to stand in this hot sun any longer and just look at me."

For Audie, peacetime brought no respite from public adulation, or from the lingering shocks of war. Constantly restless and dissatisfied, he took off for Hollywood and there began writing his war memoirs. The book, entitled *To Hell and Back* was published in 1949, and although it enjoyed brisk sales, Audie was far from pleased with it. "Even though I tried to tell the exact truth," he said, "it came out more than life size." While writing the book, he also tried his hand in the movies, but was damned with faint praise for his acting. Through his work in the studios, he met and married actress Wanda Hendrix, but their much-publicized marriage soon ended in divorce. Through it all, Murphy could not forget his debt to the service: "I have to admit I love the damned Army, it was father, mother, brother to me."

But Audie tried valiantly to lay the ghost of the war. He even gave away his medals *(overleaf)* to children of relatives, and for those who considered this disrespectful, Audie repeatedly explained that it was just the opposite, and his remarks revealed a man who was profoundly and permanently a soldier. "I didn't feel that they entirely belonged to me," he said. "My whole unit earned them, but I didn't know how to give them to the whole unit."

Second Lieutenant Audie L. Murphy, 15th Infantry, 3rd Division, 26 January 1945, near Holtzwihr, France, commanded Company B, which was attacked by six tanks and waves of infantry. Lieutenant Murphy ordered his men to withdraw to prepared positions in a woods, while he remained forward at his command post and continued to give fire directions to the artillery by telephone. Behind him, to his right, one of our tank destroyers received a direct hit and began to burn. Its crew withdrew to the woods. Lieutenant Murphy continued to direct artillery fire which killed large numbers of the advancing enemy infantry. With the enemy tanks abreast of his position, Lieutenant Murphy climbed on the burning tank destroyer, which was in danger of blowing up at any moment, and employed its .50 caliber machine gun against the enemy. He was alone and exposed to German fire from three sides, but his deadly fire killed dozens of Germans and caused their infantry attack to waver. The enemy tanks, losing infantry support, began to fall back. For an hour the Germans tried every available weapon to eliminate Lieutenant Murphy, but he continued to hold his position and wiped out a squad which was trying to creep up unnoticed on his right flank. Germans reached as close as ten yards, only to be mowed down by his fire. He received a leg wound, but ignored it and continued the single-handed fight until his ammunition was exhausted. He then made his way to his company, refused medical attention, and organized the company in a counterattack ... His directing of artillery fire wiped out many of the enemy; he killed or wounded about 50. Lieutenant Murphy's indomitable courage and his refusal to give an inch of ground saved his company from possible encirclement and destruction, and enabled it to hold the woods which had been the enemy's objective.

Audie's Medals

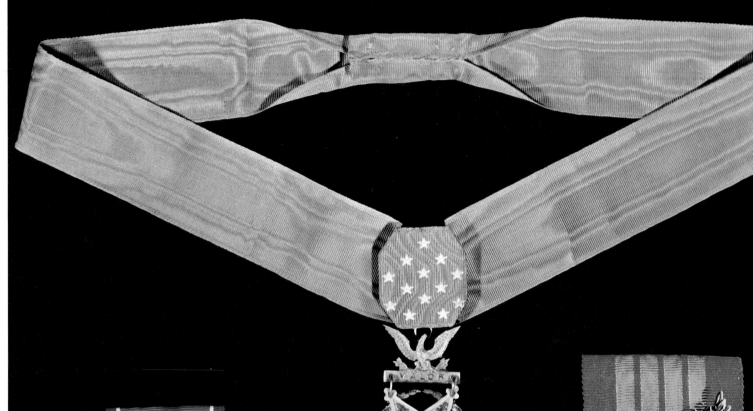

CONGRESSIONAL MEDAL OF HONOR

DISTINGUISHED SERVICE CROSS

*This array of medals made Lieutenant
Audie Murphy one of America's most decorated World
War II heroes. His more than 25 separate
citations include the Congressional Medal of Honor
and high awards from both France and Belgium.*

CROIX DE GUERRE
with palm (France)

SILVER STAR.
with oak leaf cluster

PURPLE HEART.
with oak leaf clusters

VICTORY MEDAL

EUROPEAN, AFRICAN
AND
MIDDLE EASTERN
CAMPAIGN MEDAL

BRONZE STAR
for valor, with oak leaf cluster

AMERICAN CAMPAIGN
MEDAL

LEGION OF MERIT

GOOD CONDUCT MEDAL

CROIX DE GUERRE.
with palm (Belgium)

Mail Call

Most servicemen's only contacts with home were through the letters and magazines that arrived at mail call. For men so hungry for reading matter that they would spend hours poring over the fine print on K-ration boxes, the mailbag produced treasured reminders that somewhere there was still a world of clean sheets, edible food, no duty and women. An Air Force sergeant wrote *Yank* magazine, "You can find soldiers carrying around letters so rubbed, worn and crumpled from hikes and work and general wear that they can only be read from memory. But we hold onto them." The ones they held the longest were "sugar reports" from girl friends, but any old letter would do. Millions were sent, and millions written in reply by the GIs—so many, in fact, that to save shipping space the War Department devised a miniaturized letter form known as V-mail *(below, left)*.

Every line of every kind of mail was read by a censor, who was likely to cut half the news that a serviceman wanted to give or receive. However, most veterans found ways to frustrate the censor by devising intricate family codes to pass on important tidbits. One housewife began packing whenever her Navy husband described a certain kind of seabird; the real message: his ship was due in for refitting. But the soldier who really brought the censor to his knees did so by accident—as reported by Sergeant Eugene Drucker, whose letter is among the samples at right.

I am sending you a clipping on our raid on Naples Harbour, Feb. 7. It was probably in the papers in the states but I clipped this out of the Egyptian Gazette.

Everything is fine with me, however I would sure love to get home if only for a short time, as I have been away for over a year. I am getting used to this desert life and living in a tent, and we are suffering no real hardship.

I have about 200 hours of combat time in the air in B24s which is heavy bombardment and one does get a little tired of it after a time. Even though you do get used to being shot at it does wear on a person. . . . LIEUTENANT DELBERT HALL, NORTH AFRICA, 1943

You remember the Palmer boy, who is stationed here. Well, he was up town and ran into Sgt. Arlo Fox from Spirit Lake, so he brought Arlo and his two friends down to the hospital and when I met him I remarked how sorry I was about his mother's death, and that was his first knowledge of her death in March. . . . Arlo spent the night with me and I tried to console him, but he took it mighty hard. . . . CAPTAIN DON RODAWIG, NORTH AFRICA, 1943

We have been fighting in the woods of Germany for some while now, living in fox holes and cooking our K-rations on small paper fires. The K-rations come packed in an oil-covered carton which will just about heat a canteen cup of water for your morning coffee, and believe me it certainly tastes good. But I think I'd give anything for a glass of milk and a hot meal.

While we were in France everyone was so glad to see us. They threw flowers in our path and gave us wine and fruit. All the girls kissed the soldiers, which is the French way of saying they are glad to see you—nice way, don't you think. However, in Germany there are no flowers, fruit or kisses for the Yankees and you have to watch everyone . . .

CAPTAIN MERWIN TOLLES, SOMEWHERE IN GERMANY, 1944

I thought I had been doing pretty well as far as letter-writing went, but one of the OSS guards has me beat. He claims to have written 2,827 letters (including V-mails) in his one year away from the States, and he gives no sign of slackening. To his wife he never writes less than three letters a day, and he told me that once, "just for the helluvit," he wrote her nine letters during one 12-hour guard period. I asked him how his wife took this prodigious effort and he replied: "For a while she thought it was cute but now she says she ain't got no place to keep them. She's got her bureau all full and then she started throwing them in the closet, but now she says they're leaking out." I asked him, incidentally, if he didn't think he was placing an undue strain on the censor and the mails. He thought for a moment, then replied, "Well, Jeez, it's my morale ain't it?"

In London, the poor and conscientious lieutenant who had to censor this astounding production would come in early in the morning and demand angrily, "Well, how many did you write last night?" As time went on the lieutenant became more and more upset, and on several occasions had to alter his plans for the evening in order not to get behind. One day he got very sore and barged out of his office and up to the guard desk yelling "God dammit Zicceli. I'm getting fed up with reading your goddam stupid letters! Why don't you die and dry up? I hate you and I hate your goddam wife and I hate your butcher and all the other bastards you maintain that constant diarrhea with."

According to Zicceli, the lieutenant threatened to get him transferred. Finally he WAS transferred, to Paris. Several days later, who should walk in but the lieutenant himself—transferred too. He took one look at Zicceli and groaned, "Oh my God!"

SERGEANT EUGENE P. DRUCKER, PARIS, 1944

Since seeing you in England I have sort of covered three more countries: France, Germany and Austria. I've seen what wasn't ever meant for human eyes to see. We were in Landsberg—Hitler's prison cell where he wrote "Mein Kampf." Dachau was close by. Have you ever seen stacks and piles of HUMAN bodies—200 to 300 in each pile, sprawled out, starved and beaten and gassed to death?

The only thing I've seen to compare with it was at the Landsberg camp. The evening before we moved in they had put 250 people, men and women, into this house which was sort of half dug in. The house was then saturated with gasoline and a match was all that was necessary.

The next morning we moved in under a hazy cloud of smoke. But it didn't smell like ordinary smoke. Have you ever smelled human flesh burning? That was it!!! We now have an outfit that cannot smell any sort of fire smoke without that incident and those scenes passing through his mind, because, it seems that it will never leave us, never. . . .

AN ANONYMOUS GI, SOMEWHERE IN GERMANY, 1945

In March 1945 victorious riflemen in Germany press on toward the Rhine.

It's almost over and I'm almost home and I'm scared that maybe just a
lucky shot will get me. And I don't want to die now, not
when it's almost over. I don't want to die now. Do you know what I mean?

A SOLDIER QUOTED IN *YANK—THE GI STORY OF THE WAR*

Home Front

A starred flag indicates three men in the service.

The Taxpayers' War

The town was whole. The malted milks still whirled at Bullard's store; and Oppenheimer-Stern announced their sale of new spring rayons just as sheer as nylons.   MACKINLAY KANTOR, *THE WAR IN BOONE CITY*, 1943

Every morning for four years, the first thing just about everyone did was to grab the newspaper to find out who was ahead in the war. It was easy to tell; World War II was, as TIME magazine said, "the best reported war in history." U.S. papers had at least 500 correspondents with the armed forces—five times more than in World War I. These reporters filed half a million words a day and were extraordinarily courageous: they flew in bombers through Berlin flak and rode on landing craft onto Pacific Islands and European beaches.

They did this not only because they were brave, but because the American people had a deep and perhaps guilty curiosity about the war, which was, despite all the thundering slogans, much less than a total war—and far, far away. Between the two fronts—home and battle—the contrast was enormous. At home, aside from sending sons and husbands off to fight and producing vast quantities of materiel, the war effort was mainly trivia: watching for enemy planes that never came; rationing meat, sugar and gas; trying to make do with a scarcity of hairpins and glass eyes.

Beyond that the war was, in many respects, good to non-combatants. In crucial 1943, for example, the U.S. living standard was one sixth higher than in 1939. A bombardier home on furlough in 1944 said: "Their way of life hasn't really changed a damn bit. One day I was riding on a subway and I heard one bastard say to another one, 'If this war lasts for two more years I'll be on easy street.'"

Business generally prospered, especially big business, which made itself still bigger as it wove complex new ties to the military. By 1945, of all Army and Navy dollar obligations 82 per cent were tightly held by the top 100 corporations. As wartime profits soared to new peaks, so did peacetime prospects: 31 giant companies operated half the government's $18 billion worth of new factories; afterward these companies would buy the plants for a song.

Yet the total effect of all this reached far beyond profiteering and personal pleasure. For ultimately the war was won at home, by the home front. America's guns, generals and GIs were good. But so were the enemies'. Where the U.S. was stunningly unique was in the massive financing and production of armaments, and in getting these armaments overseas. In 1942 an American officer who was methodically smothering a hill in Tunisia under artillery fire explained it all to a correspondent: "I'm letting the American taxpayer take this hill."

San Francisco Chronicle EXTRA
THE CITY'S ONLY HOME-OWNED NEWSPAPER
FOUNDED 1865—VOL. CLVIII, NO. 112 CCCC SAN FRANCISCO, SATURDAY, MAY 6, 1944 DAILY 5 CENTS, SUNDAY 15 CENTS: DAILY AND SUNDAY PER MONTH, $1.50

S. F. RATION STAMP RACKET SMASHED

OPA Uncovers Ring

Three Men Are Accused Of Stealing and Selling Gas and Ration Coupons

Bank Employe Is a Suspect; Investigators Declare Sales Were Made to Shipyard Workers

An amazing black market ring in gas coupons and ration stamps, allegedly stolen by trusted workers in a local bank, was smashed yesterday, the O. P. A. declared.

In custody, it was learned, were two Marinship employes—George Kirkham, 25, of Marin City, and Emeio J. Maionchi, 27, of 2205 Jones street, San Francisco.

Shoe coupons also were also allegedly peddled at the shipyard for $1 each. The racket, described as one of the most insidious uncovered by OPA investigators to date, operated in this manner, according to Chief Investigator Roy Danforth:

A suspected clerk of the bank, which handles the consumer-cashed ration stamps turned in by merchants and service station operators, entered the deposits in regular fashion. These gas coupons and the red and blue ration stamps are pasted onto large sheets before depositing.

The suspected clerk, OPA investigators said, after making the ledger entries, steamed off the stamps and coupons, then smuggled them out the rear door.

From that rear door, the course of the stolen stamps into the black market was traced, OPA said, through admissions by Kirkham.

KIRKHAM ARRESTED

Kirkham, they said, acted as a sort of retailer and reputedly admitted peddling some 300 coupons and stamps—gas, read and blue. He was arrested several days ago and released on bond.

Kirkham told investigators he received his illegal stamps from Maioncni, who was described as a "jobber" or intermediary for the bank clerk. Maionchi, it was stated, was picked up in the vicinity of the Marinship yard late yesterday after he had allegedly delivered additional second-hand stamps to Kirkham. He was booked at the County Jail at San Rafael as "en route" to the U. S. Marshal here.

How extensive were the operations of this "inside" ring was not immediately known. Further arrests were expected.

House Passes Simplified Tax Bill

By the Associated Press

WASHINGTON, May 5—Spurred by the national outcry against the intricacy and confusion of wartime taxation, the House passed unanimously today a bill designed to relieve some 30,000,000 of the 50,000,000 taxpayers of the necessity of computing income tax returns.

The vote was 358 to 0, the first time in the memory of House veterans that a tax bill passed without a dissenting vote.

This action shuttled the tax simplication legislation to the Senate, where Chairman George (D., Ga.) of the Finance Committee, predicted early approval.

The streamliner would:

1—Scrap the 2-year-old "Victory" tax and set new normal and surtax rates and exemptions while keeping actual tax burdens near present levels.

2—Change the withholding levy against wages and salaries—effective next January 1—to deduct currently the full tax liability of persons earning up to $5000—thus removing the necessity for 30,000,000 persons to compute formal returns.

3—Of the 20,000,000 who still would be required to file returns, 10,000,000 (those earning less than $5000 but with income other than wages and salaries) could use a simple table showing their entire tax. The remaining 10,000,000, with income over $5000, would fill out a simpler return than the present long form.

SINGLE PERSONS

The revised normal and surtaxes would be applicable for returns filed next March 15 on 1944 income.

Generally the bill would levy a somewhat larger tax against single persons and couples without children, while the load would be light-

Continued on Page 4, Col. 6

The Axis Arms

Third article in the series by Nat A. Barrows on the Axis invasion preparations will be printed in Sunday's paper.

British Face Tighter Rationing

WASHINGTON, May 5 (AP)—Great Britain, in contrast to recent developments here, is preparing for a possible tightening of food rationing and a continuation of controls for possibly two years after the war in Europe ends.

James A. Scott Watson, retiring British agricultural attache in this country, told a press conference this today, adding that his country saw little hope of normal food supplies before 1947. He ascribed a sharp difference in meat supplies of the two countries largely to the necessity of using United Nations shipping for movement of war materials and fighting men.

(AP) Wirephoto

ADMIRAL SOEMU TOYODA
He succeeds Koga as Japanese fleet commander

Drive Toward Tokyo

U. S. Planes Hit Jap Air Bases In New Guinea

By the Associated Press

ADVANCED ALLIED H. Q., Southwest Pacific, Saturday, May 6 (AP)—Allied planes have intensified their campaign on neutralizing the Schouten islands in Dutch New Guinea area where the Japanese are reported massing naval air strength, headquarters announced today.

Several enemy planes were smashed on the ground, and interceptors were driven off in a new raid on Schouten airbases which lie more than 200 miles northwest of invaded Hollandia.

That is in the sector where a spokesman said yesterday the Japanese were sending reinforcements of their well-trained naval flyers to block the westward movement of General Douglas MacArthur's forces toward the Philippines.

WEWAK HIT AGAIN

Wake island air base, the nearest one to the West of Hollandia, also was raided and neutralizing attacks were continued against Wewak to the southeast of Hollandia.

Some of the estimated 60,000 Japanese troops isolated between Hollandia and the Madang area have been noticed concentrating at Wewak.

In the Wewak-Hansa bay sector where the Nipponese have been trying to flee on barges, headquarters reported today that swift patrol torpedo boats had damaged 20 more barges and silenced three shore batteries.

Wandering groups of starving, dejected Japanese are continuing to give themselves up to the Hollandia invasion forces. A spokesman said today the total number of the enemy which has surrendered there now totals 155. Although small, that is large when contrasted with other similar operations of the past. Here-

Continued on Page 4, Col. 2

Japs' Naval Chief Koga Dies in Action

By the Associated Press

WASHINGTON, May 5—Admiral Mineichi Koga, commander of the combined Japanese fleet, was killed in action on an undisclosed front in March—the second Japanese fleet chief to die in action within a year—and has been succeeded by the colorless Admiral Soemu Toyoda, the Tokyo High Command announced today.

An imperial headquarters communique recorded by U. S. Government monitors said Koga had "died at his post in March of this year while directing operations from an airplane at the front."

It bore a striking similarity to the Tokyo communique of May 21, 1943, announcing the death of the former fleet chief, boastful Isoroku Yamamoto, in a warplane the previous April.

NO DETAILS GIVEN

Yamamoto, who once boasted he would dictate the peace terms in the White House, was known as the man who torpedoed the London naval conference in 1934 and planned the attack on Pearl Harbor. Tokyo indicated last year that he died a spectacular death

Continued on Page 3, Col. 2

Hitler Calls in Group of Envoys

LONDON, May 5 (AP)—Adolf Hitler has called to his headquarters the German envoys in neutral capitals, the Moscow radio said today. Franz von Papen already is home from Turkey, which has cut off chrome shipments to Germany. Moscow said the envoy to Spain, which is reducing wolfram shipments, had been summoned while the Minister to Stockholm, where the Allies are seeking reductions of bearing exports, also was to be called.

The War In Asia

British Open Counterdrive At Kohima

By the United Press

SOUTHEAST ASIA H. Q., Kandy, Ceylon, May 5—British troops have launched a general counter-offensive on the Kohima front and are making satisfactory progress," while in North Burma Chinese troops, led by American tanks, have captured Inkagahtawng and trapped its Japanese garrison of 1000 men, it was announced tonight.

A communique from Admiral Lord Louis Mountbatten's headquarters revealed that "our troops are attacking at all points" around Kohima, seeking to remove the threat to Eastern India.

The counter-offensive was carefully timed to strike less than two weeks before the monsoon, so that once the Japanese are dislodged from their stubbornly held positions and thrown into retreat, the weather will spur on their disaster.

POWERFUL SUPPORT

A final spell of fair weather enabled British and American planes to contribute powerful supporting attacks against Japanese communications extending to the Mandalay area, where railroad yards and military stores were blasted.

In capturing Inkagahtawng, Lieutenant General Joseph W. Stilwell's Chinese and American units gained a level route to Kaimang, 18 miles to the south across dusty paddy fields that will not be flooded for at least three weeks. Other Chinese units were only 10 miles from Kaimang at Manpin, but were outside the flat valley which provides the best approach to the Japanese stronghold.

Front dispatches said that Inkagahtawng, a strategic position rather than a town since not even one hut is situated there, fell to an American tank attack after planes had almost obliterated the enemy defenses. American P-51 Mustangs and P-40 Warhawks dumped more than 15 tons of bombs on an area 1500 yards square.

A ROAD BLOCK

Meanwhile, a Chinese flying column slipped around the Japanese positions and threw a road block across the enemy's only trail of escape at a point two miles south of Inkagahtawng. A battalion of about 1000 Japanese was trapped. Allied casualties in the entire operations were only a few men killed or wounded.

Mountbatten's communique reported only minor clashes in the Imphal area south of Kohima, where a few days ago the Japanese appeared about to launch a major attack. Allied patrols found hundreds of bodies of Japanese killed in the recent heavy fighting in that sector.

Aimee McPherson Seriously Ill

LOS ANGELES, May 5 (UP)—Evangelist Aime Semple McPherson was seriously ill at her hilltop home today, her son, Rolf McPherson, reported.

Mrs. McPherson is suffering from an infection which followed a tropical fever she contracted in Mexico and has been ill intermittently for more than a year.

21st Day of Raids

Allied Bombers Blast Huge Dam in Italy, Nazi Strongholds Periled

German Defenses Near the Adriatic Are Threatened; U. S. Heavies Hit Rail Yards at Ploesti

By the Associated Press

LONDON, May 5—American and British dive bombers of the Mediterranean command in a notable coup cracked open the huge Pescara dam in Italy this afternoon, releasing a great wall of flood water which threatened to engulf German strongholds near the Adriatic coast and sweep away bridges vital to Axis military traffic in that long-stalemated sector.

At the same time American heavy bombers striking into Romania hit rail yards at the oil center of Ploesti and at Turnu-Severin near the Danube "iron gate" on the 21st straight day of the two-way pre-invasion sky offensive which is softening up the Atlantic wall and giving direct support to the Red Army in the East.

Italy-based American bomber fleets also struck Podgorica, Yugoslavia, where a big German garrison is located.

Meantime, hundreds of U. S. Liberators and Allied planes from Britain smashed the French Calais anti-invasion defenses and strings of freight cars on rail feeder lines behind it.

ATTACK ON IRAN

Mustang and Kittyhawk fighter-bombers with American pilots in the vanguard made the attack on the Pescara dam near Torre de Passeri, 19 miles up the Pescala river from the port of the same name on the Adriatic side of the Italian peninsula opposite Rome.

The stroke ranked spectacularly with the RAF's successful attack last year on the Mohne dam in Germany.

The Pescara dam's iron sluice gates were ripped apart by underwater explosions from bombs in a 20-minute attack.

As the last Allied flyer left the scene a high wall of water followed by five even higher waves already was a mile downstream, rushing swiftly toward German-occupied Italian cities and Axis defenses erected opposite the British Eighth Army lines in the Orton sector, 10 miles below the port of Pescara.

ANOTHER BREAK

A bomb from the plane of Sergeant Alexander Duguid of Scotland apparently was the first to breach the dam, and Ken Richards, an Australian Kittyhawk pilot, saw his explosives make another break in the iron walls.

American Mustang pilots made the

Continued on Page 3, Col. 3

Nazis Pour Into Norway And Denmark

By the Associated Press

LONDON, May 5—**The Germans were reported tonight to have sent 20,000 reinforcements into restive Denmark and 30,000 into Norway in a new series of anti-invasion moves ranging along almost the entire Western front.**

Berlin radio commentators continued to discuss the expected Allied assault as being imminent.

A high percentage of seasoned veterans was included among the troops rushed to the Danish and Norwegian sectors of Germany's western defenses, said reports received here through Stockholm.

FLANDERS' FLOODS

The Belgian News Agency said the Germans had flooded the coastal zone both east and west of Flanders, inundating most roads. This flooding, the news agency added, although undertaken to check invaders, has forced the Nazis to take special protective measures with their defense works between the sea and the submerged inland regions.

Especially in the neighborhood of Calais, Dunkerque, Gravelines and Nieuport rising water and displaced sands from dunes are threatening the defense construction, it was said.

The Germans announced they were ready for assault from any direction, drawing their latest omen from Iceland with a report that there was "great Allied activity and large shipping concentrations there, reinforcing the impression that the Allies are planning an invasion of Scandinavia."

"GREAT GRAVITY"

The Paris radio saw "great gravity" in the west, and Berlin and Vichy commentators noted "mounting Allied reinforcements" in Italy and predicted a blow there simultaneously with the offensive from the west. Algiers said the Germans were rushing fortifications on the island of Elba, lying between Corsica and the Italian northwest coast.

Extortionist Faints At Long Sentence

NEW YORK, May 5 (UP)—Jacob (Gurrah) Shapiro, erstwhile tough partner of the late Louis (Lepke) Buchalter, fainted in General Sessions Court today after he was sentenced to from 15 years to life for extortion.

With tears streaming down his face, Shapiro trembled and gulped one sedative pill after another as he heard Judge John A. Mullen pass mandatory sentence on him as a fourth offender.

"Thank you, Judge, thank you," he mumbled. Attendants helped him from the courtroom and he collapsed in the lobby. A physician revived him within a few minutes.

Weather Man

"Was worried about the Army and Ward's," said Anemometer.

"Why wus you worried?" demanded the Weather Man.

"In case the Army'd get out a catalogue."

"That's part of the business."

"But how'd you know what you were buyin'? You'd get items listed like this: O B in hars, Fst stl. Solve rat prob by rsg own vegs. Or BB sted."

"What's wrg with that? It's clr as mud to me," and the W. M. cooked up a couple of isotherms and got tdy's frost: FAIR.

Black Market Whisky Trial

Union Agent Is Named as 'Go-Between'

Jack Goldberger, a union business agent and former ration board member, was named as a "go between" in the whisky black market yesterday at the trial of Frank DePaolo, liquor concern salesmanager, charged with conspiracy to sell liquor above ceiling prices.

Jack Reynolds, an Alameda county AFL union leader, has pleaded guilty to the same charge.

The name of Goldberger was brought into the case to the surprise of Assistant United States Attorney Al Zirpoli. Goldberger is not under indictment, but Zirpoli said an effort will be made to bring him into court.

Goldberger was dragged into the case in Federal Judge Welch's court by Attorney Harold Faulkner, counsel for DePaolo, in an effort to refute the Government's contention that DePaolo was active in soliciting illegal whisky deals.

William Sylvester, a member of the Newspaper and Periodical Drivers and Helpers' Union, Local 921, of which Goldberger is business agent, testifying as a witness for DePaolo, said that he had introduced Goldberger and DePaolo after Goldberger had asked him if he "knew anyone who would be interested in quite a lot of whisky."

Sylvester said he did this merely "as a favor to a friend," that there was nothing in it for him.

DePaolo later testified the transaction, involving 1500 cases of Baltimore Club Special Reserve bourbon, was subsequently completed, but denied there was a violation of the law.

The Office of Price Administration, in obtaining last year a Federal order restraining the Rolandelli Company from selling this whisky above the $27 ceiling price, claimed the liquor was sold for as much as $50 a case. DePaolo is salesmanager for this company.

DePaolo denied that he had ever known Jack Reynolds, who after pleading guilty, had testified to alleged dealings with DePaolo in illicit handling of liquor. On Thanksgiving Day, when Reynolds declared he had discussed the proposed deal with him, DePaolo asserted he was enjoying the holiday dinner with his family.

Goldberger resigned last February as a member of War Price and Ration Board No. 8.

The Index

Listen to The Chronicle-KYA Time-Clocked News—1260 on your dial—6 a. m. to midnight

Gandhi Will Be Freed Today Because of Failing Health

LONDON, May 5 (AP)—Mohardas K. Gandhi, the Indian leader, will be released from internment tomorrow morning.

A statement issued tonight simultaneously in London and India said:

"In view of medical reports of Mr. Gandhi's health, the government of India have decided to release him unconditionally. This decision has been taken solely on medical grounds. The release takes place at 8 a. m. May 6.

The 75-year-old leader in the struggle for Indian freedom has been imprisoned in the ornate palace of the Aga Khan at Poona since August, 1942, because of his attitude toward India's resistance to Japan.

He developed a fever last month less than two months after the death of his wife, and although he showed improvement his general condition caused anxiety.

For 40 years he has been a dominant figure in the life of India, called the Mahatma (Great Soul) during most of his career as a nationalist leader and variously regarded as a saint, a revolutionary and a reactionary, a patriot and an unscrupulous politician. Millions in teeming India regard him as nothing less than a god.

His favorite weapon to rouse the masses have been his fasts and his civil disobedience campaign.

The Industrial Muscle

Late in 1943, at a meeting between F.D.R., Churchill and Stalin in Teheran, the Russian leader offered a toast: "To American production, without which this war would have been lost." As Stalin spoke, Russian soldiers in U.S. trucks and jeeps were rolling the Nazis back on the 2,000-mile front. Just as toastworthy was the speed with which America had turned to the making of munitions. In 1939 only 2 per cent of the gross national output was armaments. But in the year after Pearl Harbor war production quadrupled; and by 1944 American assembly lines were spewing out 50 per cent more armaments than the Axis nations. Not all of the American production was first class: hastily welded Liberty Ships were known to break apart in heavy seas; the Sherman tank was considered more vulnerable than the German Tiger tank; and American torpedoes were notorious for malfunctioning (one frustrated U.S. submarine crew, with Japan's largest oil tanker sitting unprotected in its sights, hit the ship with eight duds before running out of ammunition). Nevertheless, most U.S. weapons were at least the equal of their Axis counterparts. And the continuing volume of production was so great that the enemy was eventually crushed beneath a weight of weaponry.

America's answer!

PRODUCTION

NO TIME TO LET LOOSE!

AMERICAN WORKER

It's a Fight to a Finish!

U.S. ARMY
OFFICIAL POSTER

SOLDIERS without guns

Identical twins Mary and Marjorie Vaughan of West Lafayette, Indiana, roll two of 2.5 billion bandages Red Cross wartime volunteers made.

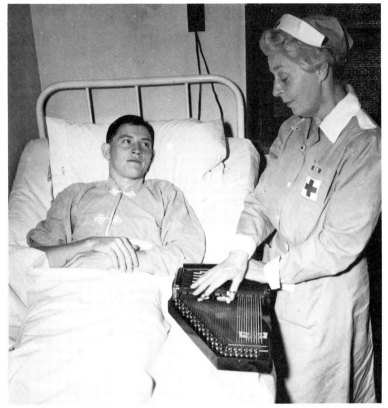

Twanging her autoharp, a Red Cross Gray Lady soothes a wounded soldier.

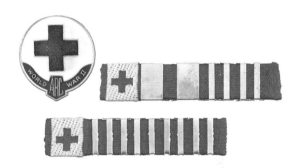

The Greatest Mother

When war suddenly fell upon the U.S., the only American organization that seemed ready to act was the Red Cross. Small wonder. The Red Cross had had 59 years of practice conducting disaster and relief programs; and with its experience in World War I—when it first called itself "The Greatest Mother" during a fund-raising drive—it was keyed to rush trained civilian aid to modern armed forces.

The day after Pearl Harbor 3,740 Red Cross chapters rallied tens of thousands of volunteers to roll bandages, amuse the wounded and carry out other merciful tasks that might help win the war. Throughout the conflict the enormous Red Cross emergency blood bank program collected 13.3 million units of blood for plasma from 6.66 million queasy volunteer donors.

The only reward Red Cross volunteers received for their millions of hours of work was the private satisfaction of doing a needed job—plus cherished Red Cross pins and service ribbons. Proudly worn over the uniform pocket, the ribbons (*above*) had stripes of silver for every 500 hours of service, thin gold stripes for 1,000 hours and wide gold stripes for 5,000 hours. The upper ribbon, worn by a small elite corps, represents a staggering 14,000 hours of Red Cross work—or 10 hours for every day of the war.

Red Cross volunteers give magazines to U.S. servicemen on a troop train.

Going by the Book

For a people almost totally unused to any kind of wartime sacrifice, WPB Directive No. 1 to OPA, January 1942 —instituting rationing—came as a shock. Suddenly, U.S. citizens were stuck with a mess of little books and stamps that limited the food or gas they could buy. What's more, the instructions on how to use the food stamps seemed incomprehensible *(below)*.

Gasoline rationing was especially unpopular. When the average driver received an "A" card limiting him to a mere three gallons of gas a week, he started to cheat. By late 1942 gas-chiseling became a national scandal but eventually most drivers turned in the extra cards they had wheedled and made do with the patriotic three gallons.

All RED and BLUE stamps in War Ration Book 4 are WORTH 10 POINTS EACH. RED and BLUE TOKENS are WORTH 1 POINT EACH. RED and BLUE TOKENS are used to make CHANGE for RED and BLUE stamps only when purchase is made. IMPORTANT! POINT VALUES of BROWN and GREEN STAMPS are NOT changed.

At seven in the morning of July 21, 1942, the day before strict gas rationing started, cars jam a Washington, D.C., gas station to fill up.

Cuts of meat, prominently marked with OPA ceiling prices and ration point values, lie displayed on the counter of a butcher shop in March 1943.

Wartime Shopping Guide

Item	Weight	Point Value
PORTERHOUSE STEAK	1 lb.	12
HAMBURGER	1 lb.	7
LOIN LAMB CHOPS	1 lb.	9
HAM	1 lb.	7
BUTTER	1 lb.	16
MARGARINE	1 lb.	4
CANNED SARDINES	1 lb.	12
CANNED MILK	1 lb.	1
AMERICAN CHEDDAR CHEESE	1 lb.	8
DRIED BEEF SLICES	1 lb.	16
PEACHES	16 oz. can	18
CARROTS	16 oz. can	6
PINEAPPLE JUICE	46 oz. can	22
BABY FOODS	4½ oz. jar	1
FROZEN FRUIT JUICES	6 oz. can	1
TOMATO CATSUP	14 oz. bottle	15

Almost everything that Americans really liked to eat —meat, coffee, butter, cheese, sugar—was strictly rationed by a point system that drove housewives and grocers crazy. Officials had devised what they thought would be a highly workable operation: the OPA issued ration books of stamps with point values and assigned specific point values to foods. Housewives paid the grocer stamps as well as cash. The grocer, to replenish his stocks, sent the stamps to his wholesaler. The wholesaler turned the stamps in at his local bank and got credit to buy more food. In practice, the system turned into a heroic snafu. Grocers had to cope with some 14 billion points a month, actually handling about 3.5 billion tiny stamps. Sometimes they ran out of the gummed sheets the government provided to stick the stamps on—causing one wholesaler to haul loose stamps to the bank in bushel baskets. Yet the wartime U.S. was fed better than ever before: in 1945, the last year of the conflict, the Department of Agriculture reported that Americans ate more food and spent more dollars on victuals than at any other time in history.

A baffled grocer puzzles over his government rationing list as he makes a valiant attempt to label his stock with the correct price in points.

The Call to Arms

Immediately after Pearl Harbor the War Department launched the greatest recruiting drive in the nation's history, and by V-J Day it had put nearly 16 million people into uniform. This thorough sweeping-up of manpower had a noticeable effect on America's way of life: men in civvies became scarce on U.S. streets and on college campuses. By the end of the fall term of 1942 three quarters of the undergraduates at Yale had enlisted; and the university had already graduated the class of 1943—six months ahead of time—in order to hustle college-deferred boys into the service faster. Most of these potential recruits searched zealously for an alternative to becoming infantrymen. They were not unpatriotic, just sure there must be more productive ways to spend the war than sitting around in a muddy foxhole with a rifle. Some enrolled in Army or Navy line-officers' training schools; others signed up claiming special vocations—like auto repairman, Russian translator or even lifeguard. A few went to extreme lengths to get into their chosen branch of the service: one high-school student in suburban Philadelphia, his heart set on being an Army fighter pilot, ate so many carrots (good for the eyes, according to contemporary belief) that his skin turned briefly but brightly orange.

IT'S A WOMAN'S WAR TOO!

JOIN THE
WAVES

YOUR COUNTRY NEEDS YOU NOW

Apply to your nearest
NAVY RECRUITING STATION OR OFFICE OF NA

Man the
GUNS
Join the NAVY

I WANT YOU

for the U.S. ARMY
ENLIST NOW

"If you've got eyes, ears, and a throat, you're in," said a barracks wit.

A recruit looks away while he gets the dreaded immunization needle.

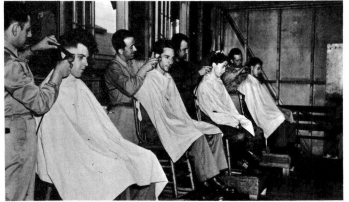

Barbers reduce luxuriant civilian hair to a Spartan one-half inch.

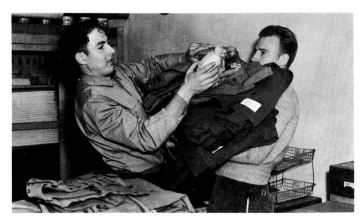

One supply sergeant told gripers, "This ain't Hart, Shaffner, or Marx."

THE SAD SACK   THE UNIFORM

SGT. GEORGE BAKER

68

Government Issue

From the very beginning of the war, the American GI was the best-equipped soldier in the world. His gear was further improved in 1942 when the chamber-pot helmet and Garand M-1 replaced the old tin hat and Springfield rifle.

LOCKER
  CAP, GARRISON
  CAP, FIELD, COTTON
  JACKET, FIELD
  SHIRT, FLANNEL
  BLOUSE, WOOL
  NECKTIE, KHAKI
  FATIGUES, BLOUSE
  AND TROUSERS
  TROUSERS, WOOL
  UNIFORMS, SUMMER, COTTON

BED (Field Equipment)
  RAINCOAT
  TENT WITH PEGS,
  POLE, ROPE
  UNDERSHIRT, DRAWERS,
  HANDKERCHIEF
  FIRST-AID POUCH
  AND PACKET
  CANTEEN COVER
  CARTRIDGE BELT
  PACK CARRIER
  HAVERSACK, OPEN
  MESS KIT
  TOILET KIT
  SOCKS
  TOWEL
  HELMET, STEEL
  ENTRENCHING TOOL
  BAYONET
  CUP
  CANTEEN
  RIFLE, SPRINGFIELD
  BLANKET, FIELD

FOOTLOCKER
  SOCKS, WOOL AND COTTON
  EXTRA TOILET ARTICLES
  UNDERWEAR,
  TOWELS,
  HANDKERCHIEFS
  SHOES, SERVICE

In 1940 cartoonist Ham Fisher's mythical boxer, Joe Palooka, joined the Army, boosting the draft so effectively that F.D.R. personally thanked Fisher.

The Funnies Fight the War ...

When American men went to war; so did American funny-paper characters.

Smilin' Jack joined the Army Air Force. Terry fought the Japanese instead

of Pirates. And while Daddy Warbucks served as a general, his adopted waif,

Little Orphan Annie, exhorted real kids to collect scrap metal.

Light Look at a Dark Time

*While Hollywood cranked out straight-faced clinkers about
the war and funny-paper artists solemnly sent their own heroes off to fight, magazine
cartoonists—especially in "Esquire" and "The New Yorker"—poked
unabashed fun at the home-front chaos of shortages, spy scares and rationing.*

"I had quite a time persuading the Smithsonian to give it back to me, as you may imagine."

"Hello, shipyard? Madam will be a bit
late punching the time clock this morning—she had
the Vanderbilts to dinner last night."

© 1943 BY ESQUIRE, INC.

"Goodbye, darling. Come home early. Remember, I
promised you for the air-raid drill tonight. You're to be a
victim pinned under a pole in front of the A.&P."

"It might be well to encourage some
talking, don't you think?"

© 1944 BY ESQUIRE, INC.

"I'm just frying the white of the egg for you, dear,
tomorrow you can have the yolk."

© 1943 BY ESQUIRE, INC.

"They're related by Red Cross blood."

© 1944 BY ESQUIRE, INC.

"We saved thirteen points sending Junior to bed without his supper."

© 1944 BY ESQUIRE, INC.

"We never thought we'd have to use these antiques
when we bought them."

© 1943 BY ESQUIRE, INC.

"So this GI goes AWOL for a coupla hours to put a fin on a gee-gee
in the sixth and the CO busts him down to a buck
—the filly comes in 20-to-1 and now the old man is trying to G-2
him for hot tips with three up and two down for bait."

© 1943 BY ESQUIRE, INC.

"He says it's not that he wants the beer so much, but they need the bottle caps for the war effort!"

After the War

Home from Europe just after V-E Day, a jubilant airman kisses U.S. soil.

The Readjustment

Has Your Husband come home to the right woman?
LADIES' HOME JOURNAL, 1945

Every serviceman had his own image of what he was going to do when he got home. Some swore they would grab the first girl they saw, and did *(right)*. Others planned to sleep for a month, getting up only for edible, home-cooked meals. Others planned to blow their separation pay on the longest binge of their lives.

But after a few days or weeks of living out such fantasies, the hero had to face up to some hard facts—how he would get a job and where he would live.

Because of wartime priorities, few new civilian dwellings had been built during the preceding years. The government had promised 2.7 million new houses by 1948, but meanwhile President Truman begged the public to find living space for veterans. The city of Atlanta bought 100 trailers for married GIs; in North Dakota, veterans turned surplus grain bins into housing; in Cleveland, Benny Goodman's band played for a benefit at which citizens pledged rooms for rent, instead of money. Getting a job turned out to be less of a problem than many had anticipated. Some veterans set up their own businesses with government loans and money they had saved in the service. Others returned to their old trades or went to college on the more than $500 yearly tuition plus living allowance ($90 a month for married men) provided by a generous law called the GI Bill of Rights. Although some veterans would always bear physical and emotional scars from the war, most were quickly caught up in the new America they discovered—the gadgets like television, the new personalities in politics and entertainment and the new fads.

But there were many people—psychologists, sociologists and just plain mothers and wives—who were determined to believe in a readjustment problem, and to solve it. Articles ran in women's magazines with titles like "What You Can Do to Help the Returning Veteran" and "Will He Be Changed?" *Good Housekeeping* said: "After two or three weeks he should be finished with talking, with oppressive remembering. If he still goes over the same stories, reveals the same emotions, you had best consult a psychiatrist. This condition is neurotic." *House Beautiful* suggested that "Home must be the greatest rehabilitation center of them all" and photographed a living room designed for a returning general. The editors also noted that Wacs and Waves, starved for feminine frills, would expect their bedrooms to be redecorated. "G.I. Jane," they solemnly stated, "will retool with ruffles."

In Times Square, a sailor grabs a girl and celebrates in his own fashion, V-J Day, August 14, 1945—the end of the war with Japan.

As the services demobilized, every discharged GI was awarded this bronze lapel button decorated with a spread eagle, irreverently dubbed "the ruptured duck."

Hubert Humphrey, elected Senator from ▶ Minnesota in November 1948, grasps tools given him by a friend with the note: "Be on the square and keep hammering away." At the Democratic National Convention Humphrey had jammed through a liberal civil-rights plank in the party platform.

Shopping for civvies, a soldier sizes up a sharp, double-breasted suit; after discharge, soldiers had 30 days before they had to get out of uniform and into civilian clothes.

In "The Best Years of Our Lives," the movie of 1946, the disabled veteran was played by Harold Russell, a former paratrooper whose hands had been blown off on D-Day.

Which Twin has the Toni?

(see answer below)

◀ The question at left introduced the home permanent to millions of women in 1947. Later the Federal Trade Commission revealed that although one of the girls had indeed given herself a home wave, both had subsequently gone to a hairdresser.

Penicillin, produced by molds like the one ▶ pictured in this laboratory dish, was first used by the military during the war; later it became available to civilians as well.

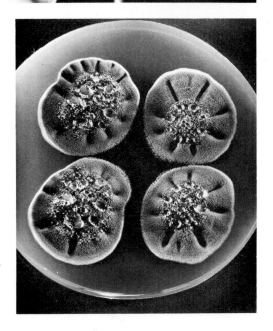

THE BEST SELLERS

◀ *Betty MacDonald gazes at the subject of her book "The Egg and I." This and the other top sellers of 1945 and 1946, listed below, reflect a postwar taste for escapism.*

FOREVER AMBER

THE ROBE

THE BLACK ROSE

BRAVE MEN

DEAR SIR

THE KING'S GENERAL

THIS SIDE OF INNOCENCE

THE RIVER ROAD

PEACE OF MIND

AS HE SAW IT

"Don't Mind Me—Just Go Right On Talking"

▲ *Eden Ahbez, composer of 1948's hit tune "Nature Boy" (below) and a conspicuous ascetic, meditates on his success in the natural environment of a cool canyon stream.*

THERE WAS A BOY,

A VERY STRANGE, ENCHANTED BOY . . .

A LITTLE SHY AND SAD OF EYE,

BUT VERY WISE WAS HE . . .

THIS HE SAID TO ME:

"THE GREATEST THING

   YOU'LL EVER LEARN

IS JUST TO LOVE

   AND BE LOVED IN RETURN."

Milton Berle was one of the regiment of ▶
vaudevillians who were rescued from oblivion by TV. As host of "The Texaco Star Theater," Berle sang, danced, did imitations and mugged—and earned $6,500 a week and the informal title of "Mr. Television."

◄ *Mrs. Clyde Smith grabs the loot she has won in a Pyramid Club. A craze in 1949, the clubs required members to pay, say, one dollar each, and recruit two others at a dollar a head. After 12 days a member theoretically won $2,048—but most clubs folded because of the decreasing mathematical probability of finding new members.*

Loafing at a Long Island soda shop, ex-GIs enjoy their membership in the "52-20 Club" named for the unemployment pay of $20 for 52 weeks granted discharged servicemen. By August 1946, six million had drawn an average of two months' benefits and General Omar Bradley, Veterans Administrator, began worrying that the boys would never get back to work. ▼

▲ *A busy carhop serves refreshments to moviegoers at one of the 2,000 drive-ins built across the country between 1947 and 1950.*

Republican Senators Arthur Vandenberg (left) and Robert Taft plan their opposition to Truman. Vandenberg dominated foreign affairs while Taft led domestic legislation. ▼

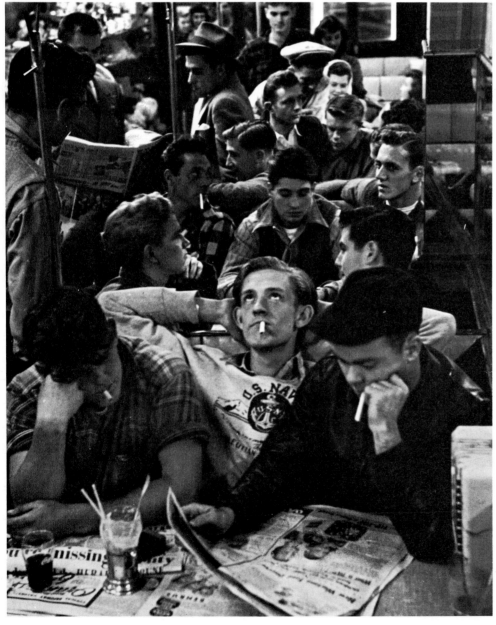

In 1950 United Nations negotiator Ralph ▶ Bunche became the first black to win the Nobel Peace Prize. Bunche received the $31,674 award for bringing an end to the Arab-Israeli war, which had broken out in major fighting on May 15, 1948.

During the fad for goopy delights like the one below, Americans gobbled up a record 714 million gallons of ice cream in 1946. ▼

▲
Vibrant Ava Gardner emerged as Hollywood's sexiest star when she appeared in films like "The Hucksters" and "Wanted."

Ed Gardner of radio's "Duffy's Tavern" started each program on the phone: "Duffy's Tavern. . . . Archie the manager speaking. Duffy ain't here. Oh, hello Duffy." ▼

By 1949 Americans were buying 100,000 ▶ television sets a week. Quiz shows and soap operas were favored by the chorebound.

TV hero to those under 13 was cowboy Hopalong Cassidy, played by William Boyd. He became so popular that "Hoppy" clothing grossed $40 million by 1950. ▼

▲
Bob Hope solos without benefit of aircraft when catapulted from a tree in one of his first postwar films, "The Paleface."

The 1948 Presidential election was the first ▶ to be shown on mass TV. The tally on the TV screen at right indicates the narrow margin by which Truman upset Dewey.

"Madman" Muntz reigned as postwar king of used-car dealers, holding to list prices to compete with a booming black market.
▼

▲
Congressman Richard Nixon fires a question during the 1948 hearings involving ex-State Department official Alger Hiss.

Though he earned almost a million dollars in 1950 as a radio and TV announcer, Arthur Godfrey often loathed commercials, as he made clear (below) during plugs. But his folksy banter prompted Fred Allen to call him "the man with the barefoot voice."
▼

HOUSING SHORTAGE

NO VACANCIES

"BE IT EVER SO HUMBLE"

THE KINSEY REPORT

Dr. Alfred C. Kinsey interviews one of the 5,300 American men whose intimate lives he explored for his 1948 bestseller, "Sexual Behavior in the Human Male." Some of his startling findings are listed below.

SEXUAL ACTIVITY AND MARRIAGE
85 per cent of married men have had pre-marital sex and 50 per cent are unfaithful.

SEXUAL ACTIVITY BY AGE
95 per cent of all males are active by 15, and maximum activity occurs at 16 or 17.

SEXUAL ACTIVITY BY OCCUPATION
Semi-skilled laborers are the most active group, men in the professions second, day laborers third, white collar workers last.

▲ *Six of 30 million "war babies" born between 1942 and 1950 scramble in a Diaper Derby at Palisades Park, New Jersey.*

◀ *Seated amid 10 years of scripts, Gertrude Berg, star and creator of the daytime serial "The Goldbergs," beams as her show graduates from radio to television in 1948. As Molly Goldberg, the Jewish mother, Gertrude Berg began every show leaning out of her window schmoozing with neighbors. Typical Goldbergisms: "Enter, whoever" and "If it's nobody, I'll call back."*

The inventor of the LP, Dr. Peter Gold-▶ mark, holds a pile of 33-rpm records containing all the music in the eight-foot tower of old 78-rpm recordings at right.

▲ Progressive Party Presidential candidate Henry Wallace grabs a quick bite during his 1948 campaign. A fourth party, the Dixiecrats, ran Strom Thurmond. Both mavericks finished far behind Truman and Dewey.

▲ The return of new cars after the war is symbolized by the showroom appearance of the 1947 Frazer. Its manufacturer, Kaiser-Frazer, was the first new company to make American cars in more than 20 years.

▲ Lithuanians arrive in America. By 1950, some 200,000 D.P.s had come to the U.S.

▲ In 1949 Russell Lynes, editor of "Harper's Magazine," divided the nation into three intellectual categories: highbrow, lowbrow and middlebrow. "Life" magazine then posed three representatives of Lynes's thesis in characteristic plumage and habitat (above). Each dressed in the clothes of his cultural station, a highbrow (left) contemplates a Picasso, a lowbrow looks at calendar art and a middlebrow studies a Grant Wood reproduction.

When his suppertime TV show for kids began, Howdy Doody sang his theme song.

IT'S HOWDY DOODY TIME.
IT'S HOWDY DOODY TIME.
BOB SMITH AND HOWDY TOO
SAY HOWDY-DOO TO YOU.

Typical of a rash of postwar girlie promotion stunts is the coronation of Barbara Hendricks of New York as "Miss Grill" for serving up 600 frankfurters in one hour.

The Senate's vituperative racist, Theodore Bilbo, who wanted all blacks deported to Liberia, called on "every red-blooded white man to use any means to keep the niggers away from the polls."

The first black to be admitted to the University of Arkansas Medical School, Edith Mae Irby waits for a class to begin. Photographer Phil Stern captures her isolation in this tense moment. Miss Irby's Admission in 1949 marked the beginning of sustained efforts to integrate colleges in the South.

Warren Austin, America's first representative to the United Nations, stands between the flags of the U.S. and the U.N.

Razzing his own product, radio comedian Henry Morgan dons earmuffs to silence the deafening racket of a breakfast cereal he is advertising. Zany and enormously popular, Morgan interviewed himself, alienated several sponsors, once auctioned off his entire radio executive staff for $83.

Singing commercials inundated the nation's postwar radio audience. "Chiquita Banana," a calypso-beat product booster, was sung 2,700 times a week at one point. The Pepsi-Cola jingle (below) was another postwar favorite, though written in 1939.

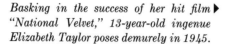

PEPSI COLA HITS THE SPOT,
TWELVE FULL OUNCES, THAT'S A LOT,
TWICE AS MUCH FOR A NICKEL TOO,
PEPSI COLA IS THE DRINK FOR YOU!
NICKEL, NICKEL, NICKEL, NICKEL,
TRICKLE, TRICKLE, TRICKLE, TRICKLE,
NICKEL, NICKEL, NICKEL, NICKEL!

Basking in the success of her hit film ▶ "National Velvet," 13-year-old ingenue Elizabeth Taylor poses demurely in 1945.

▲
Addressing the Democrats' Jefferson-Jackson Day dinner in Washington in 1948, Harry Truman, a strong advocate of civil rights, faced a table that had been reserved for—but left conspicuously empty by—segregationist Southern Democrats.

The biggest GI on any campus, Dwight Eisenhower pauses beside his wife Mamie and son John during Ike's inauguration in 1948 as president of Columbia University. Ike was one of half a million veterans who went to college after the war was over.

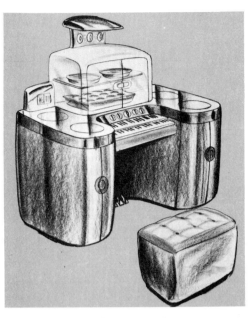

This musical stove was a purely fanciful contraption that cooked food only when its piano was played. It was created by Jean O. Reinecke—inventor of a real gadget, the electric guitar—as part of a magazine feature spoofing the boom in household machinery. The electric clothes drier was first marketed in 1946; by 1950 some 750,000 garbage disposal units had been sold, and automatic dishwashers were being purchased at a rate of 225,000 a year.

Running for his first political office, 29-year-old John F. Kennedy relaxes under his campaign poster in 1946. Kennedy won election to the House by 78,000 votes. ▶

▲ Emcee Dave Garroway ducks cotton baseballs hurled by the cast of his Chicago-based music and comedy show after he had slurred Chicago's last-place Cubs in 1949.

◀ With impassioned rhetoric, an up-and-coming evangelist named Billy Graham exhorts a crowd in Los Angeles to repent. Graham burst upon California—and the nation—in 1949 when he drew more than 300,000 people into his Los Angeles tent and converted 6,000 of them—including one notorious gangster, one cowboy singer and track star Louis Zamperini.

Moody Marlon Brando, shown tootling a recorder, was hailed in 1947 as Broadway's best young actor for his performance in "A Streetcar Named Desire." ▶

A left hook by Joe Louis sends Billy Conn to the canvas.

The End of the Long Wait

We shall miss the chaotic performances of 1945, the disorder and confusion. It will be much better baseball that we will see this year but we doubt whether it will prove either as interesting or exciting as the low-grade product of 1945.

SPORTS COLUMNIST H.G. SALSINGER, 1946

Through four long years of war, American sports fans, like American wives and sweethearts, waited for their heroes to return. In their minds were the images of departed stars—a young, lean Joe DiMaggio awaiting his next time at bat; a sleek Joe Louis stalking a challenger. But before their eyes, in wartime sports arenas, lurched a crew of has-beens and never-would-be's whose big-league incumbency was an exercise in heroic malfeasance.

Things were so bad that in the fall of 1945 sports writer Warren Brown, in assessing the two clubs that had stumbled into the World Series, predicted "I don't believe *either* team can win."

Then in 1946 the pros came back, and once again all seemed right with the sports world. Joe DiMaggio, flecks of gray now showing in his slicked-back hair, slugged 25 home runs that year. Stan Musial won the National League batting title and helped carry the Cardinals into the World Series. And Joe Louis, noting just before his long-awaited return bout with Billy Conn that the elusive challenger "can run but he can't hide," came through with the expected knockout.

While all the old heroes seemed satisfactorily the same, the games to which they returned were changing.

The traditionally white-man's world of organized baseball got its first black man. The U.S. baseball industry also got its first big scare in a long time when a Mexican millionaire named Jorge Pasquel raided the majors for talent in an abortive effort to start his own big league in Mexico. Pasquel was quickly defeated by a counterfire of U.S. dollars. But at this same time the powerful National Football League found itself faced by a very healthy newborn rival named the All-America Football Conference, which wooed players with such success that in 1950 the old league agreed to a merger.

The most important new influence on sport, however, was television. Mike Jacobs, boxing's top impresario, prophesied that title bouts would be held in empty studios for the cameras only. Many baseball and football executives agreed. Yet it soon became obvious that TV was not killing off the live fan, but rather creating a new generation of sports lovers. In 1948 the Cleveland Indians drew over 2.5 million fans, the largest game ever for a single season. By decade's end, pro football had doubled its attendance, and boxers like middleweights Tony Zale and Rocky Graziano were fighting for purses that men their size had never touched in the days before television.

Casey Stengel whoops it up with Yankee owners and players in the locker room after winning the 1949 World Series over the Brooklyn Dodgers.

"If You Were Only White"

"Many a shepherd of a limping major club has made no secret of his yearning to trade more than a couple of buttsprung outfielders for colored players of the calibre of Satchel Paige," TIME magazine reported in 1940. But there was no chance in that era of Jim Crow that any such trade would be made. Baseball, like most other major American team sports, had been lily-white since its founding days. None of the front-office men was going to risk offending the customers by putting a black player on the roster, no matter how good he might be.

Yet Leroy "Satchel" (short for Satchelfoot) Paige, along with dozens of other black athletes, had more than enough talent to make any man's ball club—as both the big-league owners and their white players discovered in off-season exhibition games. After one such exhibition in

---

SATCHEL'S RULES FOR GOOD LIVING

1. *Avoid fried foods which angry up the blood.*
2. *If your stomach disputes you, pacify it with cool thoughts.*
3. *Keep the juices flowing by jangling around gently as you move.*
4. *Go very light on the vices, such as carrying on in society, as the social ramble ain't restful.*
5. *Avoid running at all times.*
6. *Don't look back, something might be gaining on you.*

---

which Paige mowed down a row of white sluggers, Dizzy Dean, premier pitcher for the St. Louis Cardinals, declared, "Satchelfoot is worth $200,000 in any big league's money." This comment came at a time when Dean himself was paid perhaps a tenth of that.

Even as it was, Paige probably made as much as the richest white stars. Though by necessity he played most of his games in the scrubby Negro leagues, barnstorming the year round from one ramshackle stadium to another, Satch was able to parlay his enormous talents both as a player and as a promoter into an income as high as $50,000 a year. The other black stars, however, played for pea-

nuts—flavored with dubious compliments prefaced by: "If you were only white."

Ironically, when the shifting racial climate of postwar America prompted major-league teams to begin hiring blacks, it was not Paige who got the first call. That role was thrust upon a college-bred athlete named Jackie Robinson by Branch Rickey, shrewd general manager of the Brooklyn Dodgers. Rickey, who mixed a tinge of social evangelism with his baseball sense, was determined that his chosen black succeed not only as an outstanding ballplayer but as an exemplary character. Robinson had a reputation as an athlete with an explosive temper. To test his man, in their first interview Rickey suddenly called Robinson "Nigger!" He followed with a string of other ugly comments and wound up by kicking the startled athlete in the shin. Robinson kept his temper—and Rickey signed him to play for the Dodgers.

During his first season, Robinson's restraint was again tested—the St. Louis Cardinals, for example, threatened a boycott and one Cardinal tossed a black cat onto the field one day while Robinson was playing. But when the year was over, the Cardinals, who had been favored to win the pennant, were in second place; Brooklyn led the league, and Jackie Robinson, who had batted .297, was named Rookie of the Year.

With that triumph, the old barriers crashed down. The following season the major leagues had a half-dozen Negro stars, one of whom was none other than the old barnstormer himself, Satchel Paige. Though he was by now at least 40 (no one was ever sure), Paige quickly proved he had not lost his touch either as a pitcher or as a promoter. Upon signing his contract, he was asked if he thought he was capable of pitching day after day against major-league sluggers. Paige replied, "Plate's still the same size," then proceeded, in a half-season, to win six games while losing but one, helping the Cleveland Indians to a pennant. And Paige won himself thousands of additional fans through skillful manipulation of his assumed role as the wise black gypsy whose six rules for life *(above, left)* were guaranteed to bring anyone to a happy old age.

Satchel Paige rests before a game. Told he might be named Rookie of the Year, Paige replied, "Twenty-two years is a long time to be a rookie."

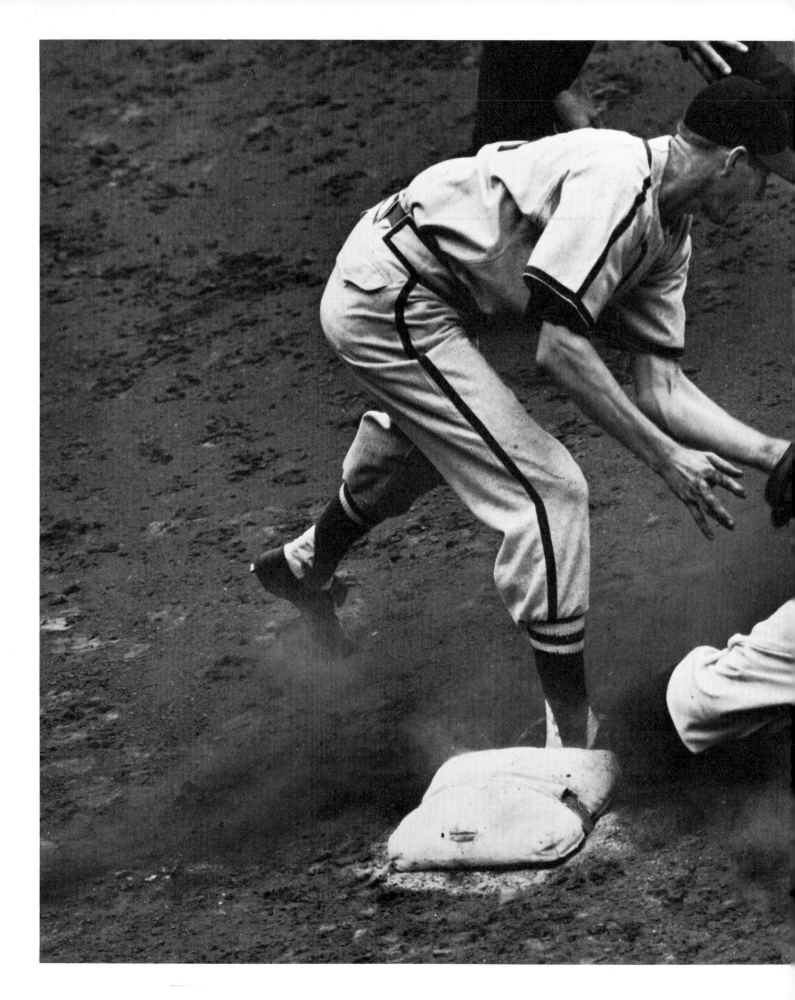

Browns fullback Marion Motley sweeps end against Pittsburgh in 1950. In this game he set a club record by averaging 17.09 yards per carry.

A sharp-shooting ring master, Sugar Ray Robinson slams a long right to the kidney as he easily overcomes a bobbing, weaving Kid Gavilan.

Boxing's Life Masters

Rarely had there been as many first-rate fighters plying their brutal trade as during the closing years of the '40s. From gentlemanly Joe Louis, model king of the heavyweights, down to pasty-faced featherweight Willie Pep, master of the blacker arts of the prize ring, virtually every division boasted not only an outstanding champion but a formidable list of challengers. Pep, for example, fought arch-rival Sandy Saddler in a series of battles that promised to stand through eternity as textbook examples of not only how to box but also how to knee, gouge, spin, grab, heel, backhand and butt while still remaining technically within the rules.

But it was the medium-sized fighters who put on the most attractive displays of premeditated violence. Dominating the welterweights was lithe, handsome Walker Smith, a graduate of the Harlem streets whose stubborn pride on such matters as segregated facilities earned him a hasty discharge from the U.S. armed forces. Under the boxing *nom de guerre* of Sugar Ray Robinson, he rolled through his bouts with such consummate ease that he was suspected of toying with even his most dangerous opponents. A New York sports writer remarked after one of Robinson's masterful, but notably restrained, performances that the champion "appeared to be round-shouldered from holding up the challenger." In the 14th round of another title defense, against flashy Kid Gavilan, Sugar Ray was so confidently in command *(left)* that he stuck out his tongue at ringsider Joe Louis, who had picked Gavilan to win. And to the erstwhile street urchin, it all seemed so easy. "Boxing's simple," he explained. "The other man can't hit you with but one hand at a time. And you got your right hand free to block that. And that leaves your own left hand free to hit him any way you want."

Such mastery of the complex science totally escaped the most exciting middleweight of the era, a wild street brawler named Rocky Graziano, who had spent part of his adolescence in solitary confinement as an incorrigible and had lost several of his boyhood friends to various forms of sudden death—including the electric chair. While being built up for a title bout in a series of matches against smaller men, Rocky explained his technique thus: "I eat up welterweights." And indeed, he did *(below)*. Then he went in against middleweight champion Tony Zale and discovered that in boxing's jungle, everybody was likely to get eaten. Through a series of three bouts that had never been equalled for sheer ferocity in the prize ring, Rocky was knocked out; then he, in turn, knocked out Zale to become champion; and finally Rocky was demolished once again in a donnybrook that led to his retirement. Even in his one winning bout with Zale, Graziano was so battered that in the ritual post-fight interview, the best thoughts he could muster were: "What? what? what? Yeah, yeah, yeah. It's marvelous. It's marvelous."

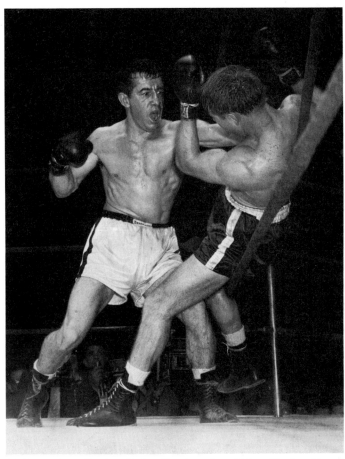

Inelegant but effective, Rocky Graziano demolishes Charley Fusari.

On September 27, 1950, boxing fans received an emotional jolt from which many of them would never quite recover *(below)*. In Yankee Stadium Joe Louis, who had retired after 12 years in which he never lost a bout as heavyweight champion, returned to the ring wars against Ezzard Charles. That night, Joe was a sad, distant cry from the catlike destroyer whose knockout punch had mowed down opponents with such terrible, swift regularity that his title defenses had become known as "The Bum of the Month Parade." Now, the erstwhile Brown Bomber was old (36) and fat (218), and a bald spot gleamed discouragingly un-der the klieg lights. Yet sentimental spectators had swallowed the myth that Charles was only a light heavyweight who had been beefed up for the event; and they hoped that Joe would somehow win—as he always had.

It was a forlorn hope, for Charles in reality was a superb, slashing boxer. He quickly took charge, and on his way to an easy, 15-round decision, had Louis holding onto the ring ropes in the 14th round. Asked later why he had not knocked out Louis then and there, Charles, a modest and notably honest man, said of his boyhood idol, "When I saw that great man helpless, I just couldn't do it."

To at least one observer, it seemed that men who sadly watched the humiliation of Joe Louis last week in Yankee Stadium were really feeling sorry for themselves. So many, in the uncomfortably long span of Louis's greatness, had themselves picked up fortyish weight and lost twentyish confidence since the first night they saw him come into New York and Yankee Stadium. And anything they felt may have been made more acute by the fact that Louis's story, in its major phase, began and ended on the same spot: the Stadium's garishly lighted, 20-by-20-foot patch of canvas. There in 1935 he had instantly excited them with their first look at his terribly swift hands, made to seem swifter by his own shuffling deliberateness and the ponderous immensity of his foe, Primo Carnera. There, only a year later, Max Schmeling found the flaw and gave him his first beating. Later Schmeling said the kid would never be able to forget it, and in a way he was right. In 1938, the German was shipped from the Stadium to a hospital after just two minutes and 4 seconds of exposure to the kid's rage.

At the Stadium, ten years later, the world heavyweight championship's longest possessor (eleven years, eight months) and most willing defender (25 bouts) preceded his retirement with one more knockout (his 51st in 61 fights). Last week, pressed for cash to settle an income-tax bill, he paid the Stadium one more visit (and made $102,840)....

For moments in the fourth and tenth rounds, Louis's left shot out with some of its remembered cobra sureness if not much of its quickness; the right followed with something of the full, overhand pitch that had rubbled so many men. He shut up Charles's left eye. But Charles turned Louis's face into a puffed, bloody lump and made him grab a ring rope in the fourteenth round to avoid falling. As a man with little experience in taking beatings (two in seventeen professional years), Louis took this one well, stubbornly marching into it. Yet referee Mark Conn could give the old champion no more than five rounds. One judge gave Charles twelve rounds; the other handed him thirteen.

A few young bloods wondered if Charles, belittled before this victory, mightn't have licked Louis the best day he ever saw. Charles himself indicated that it would take more than an hour's work (i.e., fifteen of his best rounds) to make that talk make sense. "I want to be a credit to the ring," he told an estimated television audience of 25,000,000, "just like the great champion I beat tonight." NEWSWEEK, OCTOBER 9, 1950

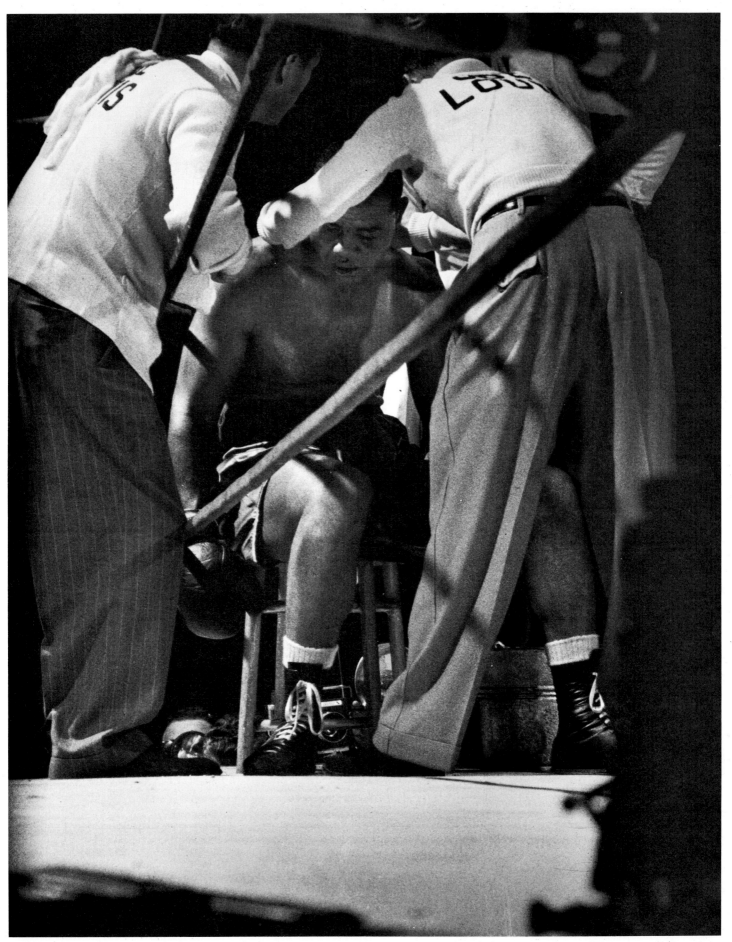

Losing to Ezzard Charles, Joe Louis slumps in his corner. Stricken fans of Louis claimed this was not the real Joe, only "what was left of him."

Theater

Mary Martin struts onstage in "South Pacific."

Oh, What a Beautiful Era

*I don't want realism. I want magic! Yes, yes, magic! I try to give that to people. I
misrepresent things to them. I don't tell the truth, I tell what ought to be the truth.
And if that is sinful, then let me be damned for it!*

BLANCHE DU BOIS IN *A STREETCAR NAMED DESIRE*

The words above might well have been the rallying cry of postwar Broadway, as the theater ushered in its brightest epoch of musical comedy and straight drama. Gone were the self-conscious political plays of the '30s that had taken the country to task for its social inequities. Gone also were dramas about war and the evils of fascism. Enter: *Annie Get Your Gun, Carousel* and *Kiss Me, Kate,* among the longest-running and most-acclaimed musicals in history. Enter, too, Arthur Miller's *Death of a Salesman* and Tennessee Williams' *A Streetcar Named Desire,* plays that analyzed people, not politics.

Broadway had to battle for this new success in a highly unfavorable climate. Never had it been more difficult to mount a production. In the '20s a lavish show had cost under $100,000; after the war, many musicals required as much as $250,000 to produce. In the season of 1928-1929 Broadway saw 200 productions; in 1949-1950, only 62 major productions appeared. Worse yet, there was a frightening rise in competition for the entertainment dollars. Television was beginning to steal audiences; sports, buoyed by the return of its prewar heroes, also drew away the crowds. When sports and television joined forces, the effect was devastating; in 1947 the World Se-

ries was telecast for the first time and Broadway reported a 50 per cent slump in business.

In the face of such hazards, many showmen became conservative, scheduling revivals of tried-and-true successes or staging low-risk adaptations of popular novels. During the period of uncertainty, lightweight comedies—like *Harvey,* starring Frank Fay, and *Born Yesterday,* which made Judy Holliday famous became the commercial mainstay of the ailing theater.

But happily, Broadway had a reservoir of new talent to overcome its woes. In the final years of the decade, musical comedies were returning profits of as much as 500 per cent. And the artistic quality of the theater had risen markedly. On January 1, 1950, Broadway song writers Richard Rodgers and Oscar Hammerstein II proudly wrote in *The New York Times:* "We believe that our modern American theater is courageous, adventurous, not dying, in fact very much alive. We have two new remarkably talented playwrights—Tennessee Williams and Arthur Miller. Two talents of their caliber rarely rise in one decade. Two are a lot. As for the American light musical theater, it is beginning to be recognized in other parts of the world as the best of its kind today."

A Streetcar Named Desire

*Marlon Brando, playing the crude Stanley Kowalski in Williams' 1947
play, manhandles the sensitive and aristocratic Blanche Du Bois, acted by Jessica Tandy.
Brando was catapulted to fame by this role, but critic Harold Clurman
complained that Brando's own "introspective, and almost lyric personality" made the
character too sympathetic and threw the production out of focus.*

A Smile Gets You No Place

ARTHUR MILLER

At 8:15 on the morning of February 11, 1949, a double file of Broadway playgoers started to line up outside the box office of the Morosco Theater on West 45th Street. Before 10:00 the ticket queue choked the sidewalks all the way down the block to Eighth Avenue. The scramble was for tickets to Arthur Miller's *Death of a Salesman*, which had just opened the night before to smash reviews. The tumult would continue through the end of 1950, when the show finally closed after winning both the Pulitzer Prize and the Drama Critics' Circle Award.

The box-office success of *Death of a Salesman* was matched by the emotional wallop the play generated. At the final curtain of its pre-Broadway debut in Philadelphia, the audience refused to go home. For almost an hour after the play ended, people stood near their seats or milled around the theater lobby, reeling from the impact of an American tragedy about an average guy—a 63-year-old traveling salesman who was at the end of the road and the end of his rope.

Willy Loman, the central character of the drama, was somebody everybody seemed to recognize. He was a man who worshiped material success, believed it came entirely by "riding on a smile and a shoeshine"—and finally killed himself. He chose suicide because he realized that he was a complete failure and that his two dearly loved sons, whom he had reared with the same set of values, had turned out to be weaklings and total failures, too.

Most Americans who came to see the play seemed to have cousins, uncles and brothers in the same boat as Willy Loman. Lee J. Cobb, the actor who played Willy for 330 grueling performances, received some 40 or 50 letters a week from people who wanted to tell him about the Willys they knew. Mature women wrote objectively but often intimately about their lives with husbands like Willy. One woman said she never understood why her husband and sons fought so bitterly until she saw Willy Loman fighting on stage with his sons. Another became so involved with the play that she wrote: "I think I shall forevermore be allergic to the words 'pull yourself together.' When you stood so forlornly on the stage after that beast told you those words and you said, 'What did I say?' my heart rushed out to you, for you were a man that was bewildered and weary and I had all I could do not to rush on the stage and give you a helping hand."

There were stacks of letters from men, too, salesmen and others, many of whom recognized either themselves or their families all too clearly in Miller's shatteringly realistic play. However, there was a hardy handful of males who managed to miss the point altogether. Wrote one such to Cobb: "I was disgusted with your appearance. Don't you ever have your pants pressed? And why don't you go on a diet?" Perhaps the most uncomprehending —and funniest—remark of all was made by a salesman who said to another as they were leaving the theater, "Well, that New England territory always was tough."

Death of a Salesman

*Lee J. Cobb as Willy Loman postures over his
sons, Cameron Mitchell as Happy, left, and Arthur Kennedy
as Biff. When Biff says he "borrowed" his
new football from the school locker room, Willy laughs: "Coach'll
probably congratulate you on your initiative."*

The RH Factor

In the summer of 1942, Richard Rodgers was feeling terrible. Although the greatest hit of his career so far, *By Jupiter*, had just opened, his lyricist and collaborator of 25 years, Lorenz Hart, was depressed and ready to quit. Hart had always been eccentric, if brilliant; he had a habit of disappearing for days at a time when he was supposed to be working on a show.

During the work on *By Jupiter*, Hart had worried himself into such a state of nerves that he checked into a hospital. Rodgers promptly moved into a nearby room, bringing along a piano in hopes of squeezing some lyrics from his partner. Somehow the songs got written, but afterward Hart gave up altogether and headed to Mexico for a rest. The timing of his departure could hardly have been worse, for a production group called the Theatre Guild was about to ask Rodgers to compose a new musical based on an old play called *Green Grow the Lilacs*.

If Rodgers' life was difficult, Oscar Hammerstein's was downright miserable. More than a decade had gone by since his last big hit; and in the past four years, he had suffered three crushing Broadway disasters. Four of the movies for which he had written lyrics had been junked, while two that were released had flopped. A Hollywood executive declared: "He can't write his hat."

At this low point, Hammerstein received a call from Rodgers asking if he might want to try some lyrics for a musical version of *Lilacs*. By sheer coincidence, Hammerstein all on his own had become interested in the musical possibilities of the same play. He had even read it aloud to Jerome Kern, hoping to form a musical partnership on the show. But Kern had turned it down, saying the play's third act was weak. Hammerstein, however, was still convinced the play was promising, and he jumped at the chance of working on it with Rodgers.

Rodgers *(seated at right)* and Hammerstein *(standing)* worked perfectly together from the start. Unlike the mercurial Hart, Hammerstein was as punctual and efficient as a Wall Street executive. And his lyrics were superb. "The very first lyric that Oscar finished," Rodgers said, "was 'Oh, What a Beautiful Mornin',' and when he handed it to me and I read it for the first time I was a little sick with joy because it was so lovely and so right."

In their unruffled and masterful way, Rodgers and Hammerstein went on to turn *Green Grow the Lilacs* into a musical called *Oklahoma!* In quick succession, they followed with *Carousel* (1945) and *South Pacific* (1949). The list of songs from each show *(below)* reads much like a hit parade of the late '40s. From a peak of success never before reached by any Broadway musical partnership, Richard Rodgers offered a modest explanation: "What happened between Oscar and me was almost chemical. Put the right components together and an explosion takes place."

OKLAHOMA!	CAROUSEL	SOUTH PACIFIC
OH, WHAT A BEAUTIFUL MORNIN'	YOU'RE A QUEER ONE, JULIE JORDAN	DITES-MOI POURQUOI
THE SURREY WITH THE FRINGE ON TOP	WHEN I MARRY MR. SNOW	A COCKEYED OPTIMIST
KANSAS CITY	IF I LOVED YOU	SOME ENCHANTED EVENING
I CAIN'T SAY NO	JUNE IS BUSTIN' OUT ALL OVER	BLOODY MARY IS THE GIRL I LOVE
MANY A NEW DAY	WHEN THE CHILDREN ARE ASLEEP	THERE IS NOTHING LIKE A DAME
IT'S A SCANDAL! IT'S AN OUTRAGE!	BLOW HIGH, BLOW LOW	BALI HA'I
PEOPLE WILL SAY	SOLILOQUY	I'M GONNA WASH THAT MAN RIGHT OUTA MY HAIR
PORE JUD	THIS WAS A REAL NICE CLAM BAKE	I'M IN LOVE WITH A WONDERFUL GUY
LONELY ROOM	GERANIUMS IN THE WINDER	YOUNGER THAN SPRINGTIME
OUT OF MY DREAMS	THERE'S NOTHIN' SO BAD FOR A WOMAN	HAPPY TALK
THE FARMER AND THE COWMAN	WHAT'S THE USE OF WOND'RIN	HONEY BUN
ALL 'ER NOTHIN'	YOU'LL NEVER WALK ALONE	YOU'VE GOT TO BE TAUGHT
OKLAHOMA!	THE HIGHEST JUDGE OF ALL	THIS NEARLY WAS MINE

In the months before *Oklahoma!* arrived on Broadway, no show ever seemed less likely to succeed. The original play, *Green Grow the Lilacs*, had run for only 64 performances when it was first produced in 1931. For its musical reincarnation, the director chosen was Rouben Mamoulian, who had worked on only one musical previously—and that had flopped. There were no stars, little racy humor and none of the splashy chorus-girl numbers that had always been considered the backbone of a Broadway musical.

Raising money for such an unlikely production was slow and agonizing. At auditions set up to lure backers, Rodgers played the score on the piano and Hammerstein narrated the plot. The results were dismal. At two auditions not a single dollar was raised (one guest commented he never did like plays about farmers). Those who did contribute money did so only as a favor to the Guild or to Rodgers and Hammerstein. But slowly the money dribbled in and the musical managed to get into rehearsal. Under the provisional title *Away We Go*, it opened in New Haven and one New York sharpie carried the verdict back to Broadway: "No Girls, No Gags, No Chance." Newly christened *Oklahoma!*, it next went to Boston, where some of the cast came down with measles and had to wear thick layers of makeup to hide their spots. When the production finally limped into New York, there were empty seats at the opening-night performance and the first public reaction came from a radio critic who predicted the show would not last a week.

The rest of New York thought otherwise. The most cautious commentary came from the *New York Herald Tribune*, which called it "a jubilant and enchanting musical." The

Oklahoma!

*A cowboy and his girl leap in one of the dances
by Agnes de Mille, a ballet choreographer. In its review, "Time"
said: "Even run-of-de-Mille dances have more style
and imaginativeness than most Broadway routines, while
the best are almost in a different world."*

New York World-Telegram proclaimed that Rodgers had written "one of the finest musical scores any musical play ever had," and LIFE declared flatly it was "Broadway's most enchanting show." The verdict of the sharpies was changed to: "No Girls, No Gags, No Tickets." When *Oklahoma!* finally closed in 1948, it had played 2,248 performances, a record for musicals. Within a few more years, each investor who had put $1,500 into the original kitty had already received back $50,000.

Oklahoma! turned the pickup partnership of Rodgers and Hammerstein into a major musical industry. The recordings from *Oklahoma!* (the first album ever to be made by the original cast of a Broadway show) sold over a million copies. While the royalties were still rolling in, the partners scored their second Broadway hit with *Carousel.* Meanwhile they set up their own production company to present other people's plays and musicals. Finally, in April 1949, they climaxed their collaboration with their own finest show, *South Pacific (left).*

Based on novelist James A. Michener's book *Tales of the South Pacific,* Hammerstein's script set the musical story on an island in the Pacific during World War II. The plot told of the love of an American Navy nurse, Nellie Forbush, and a French planter, Émile de Becque. To play the part of De Becque, Rodgers and Hammerstein signed the Metropolitan Opera basso, Ezio Pinza, who sensed a turning point in his career and wanted to try a musical. Then they approached Mary Martin and asked her to play Nellie. Her spoken reaction was, "Why do you need two basses!"—a flippant reference to her own deep alto voice. But truthfully she was terrified at the idea of singing in du-

ets opposite Pinza, with his huge, trained, operatic voice.

"I've thought it out carefully, Mary," Rodgers reassured her. "You will never have to sing with Pinza in *opposition* to him. You'll sing in *contrast* to him." This was not just empty persuasion. For De Becque, Rodgers wrote powerful, romantic melodies—"Some Enchanted Evening" and "This Nearly Was Mine." Mary Martin's much thinner voice and Nellie's gee-whizzy personality were perfectly matched in "A Cockeyed Optimist" and "I'm in Love with a Wonderful Guy."

Mary Martin signed, the show went into rehearsal and the public's interest began to build. By the time the production opened in New York on April 7, 1949, the advance ticket sales totaled nearly a million dollars. The expectations were all justified. On opening night a correspondent for the London *Evening Standard* declared, "The only thing to do is take off one's hat, borrow an expressive old Americanism, and say 'Wow!' "

The success of Rodgers and Hammerstein in producing beautifully unified shows inspired other composers. Old-timers like Irving Berlin and Cole Porter—and the new team of Alan Jay Lerner and Frederick Loewe—abandoned the grab-bag way of doing musicals, emulated the new, integrated approach and, as a result, wrote three of the best shows ever: *Annie Get Your Gun; Kiss Me, Kate;* and *Brigadoon.* As Porter remarked, "The most profound change in forty years of musical comedy has been—Rodgers and Hammerstein." That change was indeed so profound that it helped make the '40s the most successful decade in the history of Broadway musicals.

South Pacific

Mary Martin, playing a Navy nurse dressed up
for an amateur show, clowns with Seabee Luther Billis (Myron
McCormick). For her role, Miss Martin had
to stand under a shower eight shows a week to sing "I'm Gonna
Wash That Man Right Outa My Hair."

Brigadoon

*Highlanders celebrate a wedding in a mythical Scottish town
that appears for a single day every hundred years. With songs by Frederick Loewe and
Alan Jay Lerner, and choreography by Agnes de Mille, "Brigadoon"
won the Drama Critics' Circle Award for the best musical show of 1947; the score included
"Almost Like Being in Love" and "Come to Me, Bend to Me."*

119

Personalities

Sex queen Marilyn Monroe curls up languidly.

Living Symbols of an Era

I like Ike, too. ADLAI E. STEVENSON

In the fast-changing '50s, Americans quickly raised up new heroes and brought old ones crashing down. A Baptist minister, Martin Luther King, helped organize a bus boycott in Montgomery, Alabama, and emerged as spokesman of the burgeoning black civil rights movement. The young actor James Dean made a movie, *Rebel Without A Cause,* and became a symbol for his generation. Atomic scientist J. Robert Oppenheimer entered the decade a hero, but within three years his character had been cast in doubt by witch-hunting bureaucrats.

Amid these vicissitudes of fame, the foremost personality of the decade maintained his phenomenal hold on the country's affections. He was Dwight D. Eisenhower, the vastly appealing man whose radiant grin was said to be "worth 10 divisions" in war and turned out to be worth a record 33 million votes in time of peace. As one Pennsylvania housewife said when Ike was elected President in 1952: "It's like America has come home."

Coming home to politics as a 61-year-old novice after 40 years in the Army, Ike nonplussed his rivals. Senator Taft, who lost the 1952 Republican Presidential nomination to the General, found Ike's politics so vague as to be unassailable; a frustrated Taft man said in

despair, "It looks like he's pretty much for home, mother and heaven." And though the nation's leading Democrat, Adlai Stevenson, admitted *(above)* that he could not help being fond of Eisenhower, most liberals and intellectuals did not like Ike. They attacked him for failing to announce support for the Supreme Court's "deliberate speed" decision on school integration and deplored his unabashed friendship with business tycoons: "All his golfing pals are rich men he has met since 1945," groused rich young Senator Jack Kennedy.

But Ike sailed serenely forward, obviously enjoying the role of a home-grown, open-minded moderate. Moreover, there was some evidence that his platitudes and circumlocutions derived less from fuzzy thinking than from political shrewdness. Once, when Ike's press secretary, Jim Hagerty, warned that reporters might ask a sensitive question, Ike reassured him. "If that question comes up," he said, "I'll just confuse them."

But to most people it did not matter that Ike appeared noncommittal; they felt they knew what he meant and liked him for it. And that was good enough for Ike, who declared he wanted nothing more than that Americans say, "He has been fair. He has been my friend."

On vacation from the White House, Ike goes fishing with his seven-year-old grandson David on the Fraser River in Fraser, Colorado.

Sad, bad James Dean smolders with the lonesome appeal that won him the ultimate teen-age accolade: "Everything he said was cool."

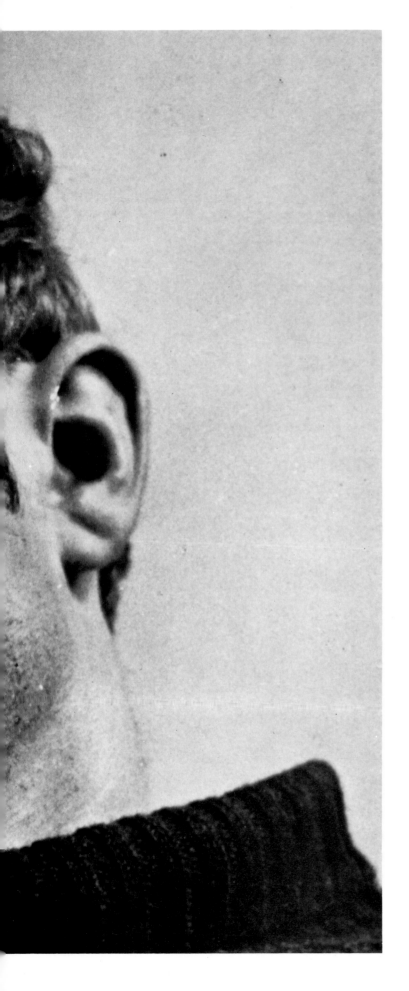

The Lost Boy

James Dean was every teen-age boy's inner vision of himself, and every girl's dream. His image was summed up by the title of his most famous movie, *Rebel Without A Cause,* in which he played the sensitive adolescent fighting a world of conformity. When he was killed in his car, at dusk on September 30, 1955, the kids made his ghost the focal point of their rebellion; their passion for him is analyzed below by novelist John Dos Passos.

There is nothing much deader
than a dead motion picture actor, and yet,
even after James Dean had been some years dead,
  when they filed out of the close darkness
and the breathedout air of the second and third
and fourth run motion picture theatres
where they'd been seeing James Dean's old films,
they still lined up:
  the boys in the jackboots and the leather jackets,
the boys in the skintight jeans, the boys in broad
motorbike belts, before the mirrors in the restroom
to look at themselves and see James Dean;
  the resentful hair, the deep eyes
floating in lonesomeness, the bitter heat look,
the scorn on the lip. . . .
  The girls flocked out dizzy with wanting
to run their fingers through his hair,
to feel that thwarted maleness; girl-boy almost,
but he needs a shave . . .
"Just him and me in the back seat of a car."
  Their fathers snort, but sometimes they remember:
"Nobody understood me either. I might have amounted
to something if the folks had understood."
The older women struggle from their seats weteyed.

The Embattled Hero

In June 1950 North Korean troops invaded South Korea, and the U.S.—and the U.N.—rallied to South Korea's defense. Americans nodded with confident approval as General Douglas MacArthur, the great hero of the Pacific in World War II and later supreme commander of the occupation troops in Japan, was appointed commander of the United Nations forces. Ten months later, Americans reacted with shock when MacArthur, having flouted U.S. policy by publicly advocating the bombing and blockading of Communist China, was summarily removed from his command by President Truman. Already frustrated and divided by the costly victory-less Korean "police action," the nation and its hard-pressed leaders lined up in two ranks, pro-MacArthur and anti-MacArthur.

The partisans were at full cry (below) when the General, calm and imperious, arrived home to find the people of the country in the throes of an emotional binge of which he was the focal point. Everywhere he went, vast crowds cheered him, and millions of people turned on their TV sets for his dramatic address to Congress. " 'Old soldiers never die,' " MacArthur intoned at the end, " 'they just fade away.' And like the old soldier of that ballad, I now close my military career and just fade away—an old soldier who tried to do his duty as God gave him the light to see that duty. Goodbye." It was good theater, and many people urged MacArthur to press ahead with a bid for the Presidency. But true to his word, he did fade—into the board of directors of Sperry-Rand—as a Senatorial hearing confirmed Truman's position that the General had ventured into the area of policy where only civilians should tread.

I believe we must try to limit the war to Korea for these vital reasons: to make sure that the precious lives of our fighting men are not wasted; to see that the security of our country and the free world is not needlessly jeopardized; and to prevent a third world war.

A number of events have made it evident that General MacArthur did not agree with that policy. I have therefore considered it essential to relieve General MacArthur so that there would be no doubt or confusion as to the real purpose and aim of our policy.

PRESIDENT HARRY S. TRUMAN

When you put on a uniform, there are certain inhibitions which you accept.

GENERAL DWIGHT D. EISENHOWER

In the opinion of the Joint Chiefs, [MacArthur's] strategy would involve us in the wrong war, at the wrong place, at the wrong time and with the wrong enemy.

GENERAL OMAR BRADLEY

His dismissal by the President is the culmination of disastrous failure of leadership in Washington.

GOVERNOR THOMAS E. DEWEY, NEW YORK

If MacArthur had his way, not one Asian would have believed the U.S. has a civilian government.

SOCIALIST NORMAN THOMAS

I do not think a general should make policies.

MRS. ELEANOR ROOSEVELT

Our only choice is to impeach President Truman.

SENATOR WILLIAM JENNER, INDIANA

We must never give up that the military is subject to and under control of the civilian administration.

SPEAKER OF THE HOUSE SAM RAYBURN, TEXAS

President Truman has given [the Communists] just what they were after—MacArthur's scalp.

SENATOR RICHARD M. NIXON, CALIFORNIA

A strong pillar in our Asian defense has been removed.

FORMER PRESIDENT HERBERT HOOVER

Snapping out orders during the brilliant Inchon landing, General Douglas MacArthur reaches his high point as Allied commander in Korea.

The Quiz Fizz

Charles Van Doren seemed perfect for the part of U.S. folk hero of the '50s. He was handsome, slim and loose-limbed in the all-American way; he was an English instructor at Columbia University at a time when teaching was becoming fashionable; and although he belonged to an eminent literary family, he was not above using high-style braininess to fight for some of the new money floating around in a decade of affluence.

The arena for Van Doren's heroics was the richest of the TV quiz shows, *Twenty-One*, on which two contestants were matched against each other on a ladder of questions. If a player missed, he was out. But if he answered correctly and chose to keep going, the questions got trickier and the payoff astronomical.

Van Doren hung on through the toughest questions, knocked off all rivals and received an all-time record payoff of $129,000. En route he won the devotion of 25 million televiewers who suffered with him as he struggled to name the only three baseball players who had made more than 3,500 hits ("Ty Cobb, Cap Anson and . . . Tris Speaker") and to pinpoint the operatic character who sings the aria "Sempre libera" in *La Traviata* ("She sings it right at the end of the party given by . . . What's her name! Soprano. Her name is . . . Violetta"). Teachers showered him with letters of thanks for proving that a hard-working pupil could master even the toughest questions; mothers instructed their daughters to marry a boy like him, not like Elvis Presley.

But at decade's end, the gold-plated world of quiz shows came crashing down. In August 1958 one of Van Doren's defeated rivals, Herbert Stempel, told the New York District Attorney's office that the show was a fake; *Twenty-One* contestants were primed with answers until their popularity began to wane. A check of other quiz programs opened an eel-bucket of fraud so tangled that a Congressional subcommittee haled witnesses down to Washington to testify. There, Van Doren put on his last performance. But this time very few Americans cared to suffer with him as he groped to explain *(below)* why a man would sell himself out.

I *would give almost anything I have to reverse the course of my life in the last three years. I cannot take back one word or action; the past does not change for anyone. But I have learned a lot in those three years. I've learned a lot about good and evil. They are not always what they appear to be. I was involved, deeply involved, in a deception. Before my first actual appearance on "Twenty-One," I was asked by Albert Freedman [producer of the show] to come to his apartment . . . . He asked me if, as a favor to him, I would agree to an arrangement whereby I would increase the entertainment value of the program. He told me that giving help to quiz contestants was merely a part of show business. This was not true but perhaps I wanted to believe him. I was sick at heart. Yet the fact is that I unfortunately agreed, after some time, to his proposal. As time went on, the show ballooned beyond my wildest expectations. I had supposed I would win a few thousand dollars and be known to a small television audience. But from an unknown college instructor I became a national celebrity. . . . To a certain extent, this went to my head. I was almost able to convince myself that it did not matter what I was doing because it was having such a good effect on the national attitude to teachers, education and the intellectual life. At the same time I was winning more money than I had ever had or even dreamed of having. I was able to convince myself that I could make up for it after it was over.*

CONGRESSIONAL SUBCOMMITTEE HEARING, NOVEMBER 2, 1959

In a soundproof booth on the TV quiz show "Twenty-One," Charles Van Doren pretends to grope for an answer he was given earlier.

because when it comes
to lingerie I want
all the luxury
but none of the fuss

it's nylon.....

...or nothing

Modess.... *because*

Connoisseur's Choice...bracelets in the Golden Manner of Monet

Monet
master jeweler
at fine stores

Everygirl

The girl that every girl wanted to be was a zestful red-headed model named Suzy Parker. Suzy was a nonstop talker whose favorite subjects were herself and her sister, mannequin Dorian Leigh. Her modeling score for the decade was over 60 magazine covers and thousands of advertisements that paid her $100,000 a year. Suzy's appeal went beyond mere beauty. She had a chameleon-like quality of looking just right in any clothes in any setting—slinky red sequins for a *Life* cover or a couple of pillows and not much else for a nylon ad. In whatever guise, she gave off an air of repressed excitement, as one fashion editor put it, "like a girl you catch a glimpse of between planes at Gander, Newfoundland, wearing a trench coat." Most of the time, Suzy seemed just as caught up by the excitement as everyone else, as these unabashed comments by Suzy on Suzy indicate.

ON HER VERY PROPER TEXAS BACKGROUND: *I come from an average Ku Klux Klan family. Actually, I was really adopted by my sister Dorian's weird parents. I'm really the lost daughter of the Dauphin. I have royal blood in my veins, and that's why I always wear Royal Blue....*

ON SUCH IMAGINATIVE STORIES: *I don't tell lies. I merely embellish stories . . . the truth is so dull.*

ON GOD'S GREAT WORKS: *I thank God for high cheekbones every time I look in the mirror in the morning.*

The Egghead

At the Democratic Convention in 1952, Governor Adlai Stevenson of Illinois was a dark-horse candidate for the Presidency, strong in the party's ruling councils and in his own pivotal state of Illinois. As such, he was a natural choice to make the convention's welcoming address, which turned out to be a brilliant exercise both in political philosophy and phrase-making. America suddenly found herself with a candidate who was running on an intellectual ticket—and even winning many supporters from the G.O.P.'s homespun Dwight Eisenhower. One of Ike's backers described a typical supporter of the Governor as having "a large oval head, faceless, unemotional, but a little bit haughty and condescending." From this description came a graphic new synonym for any intellectual—"egghead." And Stevenson became the spiritual leader for all those who felt they fitted that mold. Throughout the 1952 campaign and for much of a reprise in 1956, his speeches *(excerpted below)* were high-minded and challenging, with a counterpoint of humor. But a war-weary country wanting respite and simple solutions twice rejected his candidacy overwhelmingly.

ON FREEDOM: *Tyranny is the normal pattern of government. It is only by intense thought, by great effort, by burning idealism and unlimited sacrifice that freedom has prevailed as a system of government. And the efforts which were first necessary to create it are fully as necessary to sustain it in our own day. He who offers this thing called freedom as the soft option is a deceiver or himself deceived. He who sells it cheap or offers it as the by-product of this or that economic system is knave or fool.*

ON EDUCATION: *The softness which has crept into our educational system is a reflection of something much broader, of a national complacency, of a confusion of priorities. . . . We have lacked, I fear, the deep inner conviction that education in its broadest sense unlocks the door of our future, and that it gives us the tools without which "the pursuit of happiness" becomes a hollow chasing after triviality, a mindless boredom relieved only by the stimulus of sensationalism or quenched with a tranquilizer pill.*

ON A CANDIDATE'S DAILY ORDEALS: *You must emerge, bright and bubbling with wisdom and well-being, every morning at 8 o'clock, just in time for a charming and profound breakfast talk, shake hands with hundreds, often thousands, of people, make several "newsworthy" speeches during the day, confer with political leaders along the way and with your staff all the time, ride through city after city on the back of an open car, smiling until your mouth is dehydrated by the wind, waving until the blood runs out of your arm, and then bounce gaily, confidently, masterfully, into great howling halls, shaved and all made up for television.*

ON HIS FUTURE AFTER DEFEAT IN 1952: *There are those who feel that I should devote my talents to the welfare of mankind by frequent talking. There is another smaller group who insist that God, and/or the electorate, has appointed me the scourge of the Republican Party. And finally there is a much smaller group that feels it is not unworthy or improper to earn a living. My sons are numbered in the latter group.*

Governor Adlai E. Stevenson gathers his thoughts—and his strength—during a peaceful visit to his family farm in Libertyville, Illinois.

133

The Apostle of Nonviolence

In Montgomery, Alabama, on December 1, 1955, an act of quiet courage reshaped the career of Martin Luther King Jr., a scholarly young preacher recently installed in his first church. That day a weary black seamstress defied local law and refused to give up her bus seat to a white man. Her arrest was the last straw for Montgomery's black community; their leaders, including Dr. King, met to organize a one-day bus boycott.

On December 5, fully 90 per cent of the black populace walked or hitchhiked, but white authorities refused to budge and the blacks' mild demands escalated into an all-out campaign for desegregated public transporta-tion. King and his co-organizers set up a 200-car motor pool and underwrote the cost of their jitneys by raising about $225,000 in donations. And the blacks honored King's pleas for nonviolence *(excerpted below)*, despite arrests and harassments, capped by the bombing of King's home on January 30, 1956.

The boycott was almost a year old when, on November 13, 1956, the Supreme Court declared bus segregation illegal in Alabama. But despite this step on the road to equality, King's followers remembered his call for even greater effort: "If I am stopped, this movement will not stop, because God is with the movement."

ON PROTEST: *Nonviolence is the most potent technique for oppressed people. Unearned suffering is redemptive.*

ON VOTING RIGHTS: *All types of conniving methods are still being used to prevent Negroes from becoming regis-tered voters. The denial of this right is a betrayal of the highest mandates of our democratic traditions. So our most urgent request to the President of the United States and every member of Congress is to give us the right to vote. Give us the ballot and we will no longer have to worry the federal government about our basic rights. Give us the ballot and we will no longer plead for passage of an anti-lynching law. Give us the ballot and we will transform the salient misdeeds of bloodthirsty mobs into the calculated good deeds of orderly citizens. Give us the ballot and we will fill the legislative halls with men of good will. Give us the ballot and we will place judges on the benches of the south who will do justly and love mercy and we will place at the head of the southern states governors who have felt not only the tang of the human but also the glow of the divine.*

ON INTEGRATION: *If we are arrested every day, if we are exploited every day, if we are trampled over every day, don't ever let anyone pull you so low as to hate. There is an element of God in every man.*

ON SEGREGATION: *Many [uneducated Negroes] uncon-sciously wondered whether they deserved better condi-tions. Their minds were so conditioned to segregation that they submissively adjusted to things as they were. This is the ultimate tragedy of segregation. It not only harms one physically but injures one spiritually.*

ON CIVIL DISOBEDIENCE: *I was proud of my crime. It was the crime of joining my people in a nonviolent protest against injustice. It was the crime of seeking to instill within my people a sense of dignity and self-respect. It was the crime of desiring for my people the unalienable rights of life, liberty, and the pursuit of happiness. It was above all the crime of seeking to convince my peo-ple that noncooperation with evil is just as much a moral duty as cooperation with good.*

Dr. Martin Luther King preaches his gospel of equality and nonviolence, giving the civil rights movement a new, nationwide impetus.

Fads

Viewers gawk through Polaroid glasses at a 3-D movie.

Davy, Deepies and Ducktails

The next person who mentions Davy Crockett to me
gets a Davy Crockett flintlock over his head.

A DEPARTMENT STORE BUYER

Against a grim backdrop of the cold war and the space race, dozens of dizzy fads bubbled up in the '50s. A few of these, such as the building of bomb shelters and the sighting of mysterious flying saucers, were generated by the world news itself. Others, like ducktail haircuts and the college-bred nonsense of jamming dozens of people into a phone booth, were simply products of youth.

Some fads, however, were a product, period. In 1952 the movie industry, its audience cut in half by TV competition, was groping for a gimmick to get people back into the theaters when the Natural Vision Corporation came up with a hot idea called 3-D, or deepies. These were movies that gave a three-dimensional effect by simultaneously projecting two overlapping images, viewed by the audience through Polaroid glasses that refocused the two impressions into a single object.

The first full-length deepie, *Bwana Devil*, which premiered in Los Angeles on November 26, 1952, broke box-office records in its first week by grossing $95,000. Critics agreed that the script was awful (man-eating lions harass railroad builders in Africa), but the public loved the optical illusion of beasts that seemed to leap right out of the screen. To film makers who had doubted that people would go to movies where they had to wear special glasses, Bill Thomas of Paramount replied, "They'll wear toilet seats around their necks if you give 'em what they want to see!" But Thomas' optimism proved short-lived. The fad soon collapsed from the weight of its own dreary plots and by year's end the film trade conceded that 3-D stood for dead, dead, dead.

Meanwhile TV was generating some fads of its own, the most memorable being the cult of Davy Crockett. This one started on December 15, 1954, when an audience of 40 million (mostly between the ages of five and 15) watched lanky Fess Parker portray Davy on Walt Disney's weekly show *Disneyland.* Parker's folksy performance created a $100 million market for coonskin caps, Davy Crockett bathing suits, school lunch boxes and guitars. A record entitled "The Ballad of Davy Crockett" sold four million copies; and a merchant, stuck with 200,000 pup tents, stenciled Davy Crockett on them and sold them all in two days. But by July 1955, Davy's bull market turned b'arish; Crockett items began to pile up in stores, to the dismay of salesmen, one of whom lamented, "Kids are more fickle than women."

A four-year-old Davy Crockett checks out his coonskin cap. During the Crockett boom the price of coonskins soared to $8.00 a pound.

Cram Courses

*An outlandish spring rite called cramming—or, less
elegantly, stuffing—swept college campuses in the late '50s. The idea of the game
was to scrunch as many people or objects as possible into some small
space. It could even be done underwater—each of seven men from Fresno State held
his breath long enough to jam into a booth sunk in a swimming pool.*

Twenty-two California collegians pack into an outdoor phone booth.

Two Caltech boys adjust to a room stuffed with newspapers.

Forty students bulge out of a VW.

A Dizzying Success

In 1958 two California toy makers
heard about gym classes in Australia where kids
exercised with bamboo hoops and loved it.
Seizing upon the idea, their company, Wham-O,
began selling $1.98 plastic rings
called Hula-Hoops. Within six months American
kids were spinning 30 million
hoops put out by Wham-O and 40 imitators.

Kids compete in a Hula-Hoop derby at New Jersey's Brookside Swim Club. A 10-year-old boy set the club record at 3,000 spins.

The Big Boom's Reverberations

Americans reacted to the reality of atomic power in widely differing ways.
The adventurous bought prospectors' kits and rushed off to the Colorado Plateau or the wilds of
Canada hoping for a strike of uranium. The timorous dug bomb shelters or bought prefab
ones, against the expected nuclear attack from Russia. Neither group made out very well. Few U.S.
ore-seekers made individual finds worth $100,000 or more. And shelter-owners
found little use for their expensive caves beyond storage of garden tools and old snow tires.

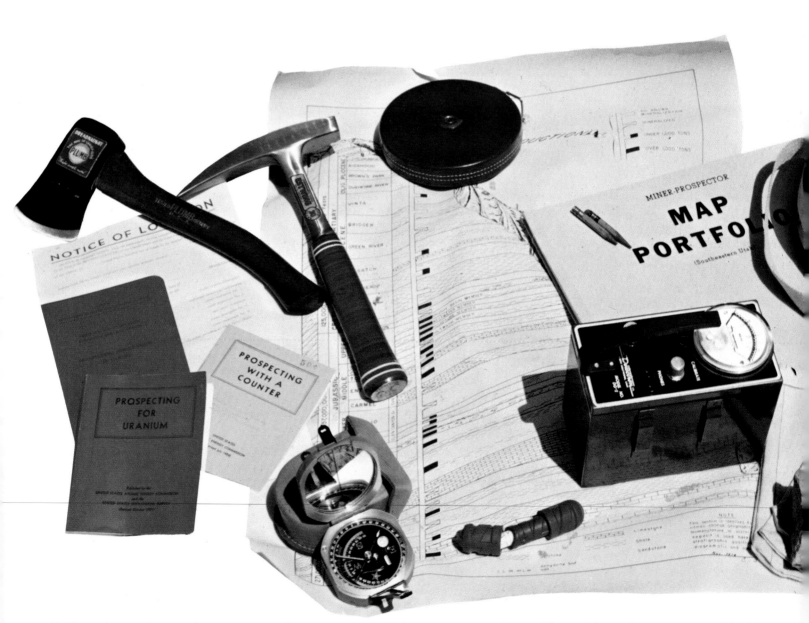

Basic equipment for uranium prospectors included a $98.50 Geiger counter, sample ore, blank claim notices and a snakebite kit.

Equipment and Supplies Inventory

THREE-WAY PORTABLE RADIO	MATTRESSES AND BLANKETS (5)
AIR BLOWER by generator or by hand	AIR PUMP for blowing up mattresses
RADIATION DETECTOR	INCANDESCENT BULBS (2) 40 watts
PROTECTIVE APPAREL SUIT	FUSES (2) 5 amperes
FACE RESPIRATOR	CLOCK nonelectric
RADIATION CHARTS (4)	FIRST AID KIT
PICK AND SHOVEL COMBINATION for digging out after blast	FLASHLIGHT
GASOLINE DRIVEN GENERATOR	WATERLESS HAND CLEANER
GASOLINE 10 gallons	STERNO STOVE
CHEMICAL TOILET	CANNED WATER 10 gallons
TOILET CHEMICAL 2 gallons	CANNED FOOD meat, powdered milk, cereal, sugar etc.
BUNKS (5)	PAPER PRODUCTS

Above is a list of articles found in the $3,000 Mark I Kidde Kokoon. This shelter came with everything a family of five might need for a three- to five-day underground stay.

Some people bought commercial shelters; others designed their own.

City's Proposal for Air Raid Shelter in Private Homes

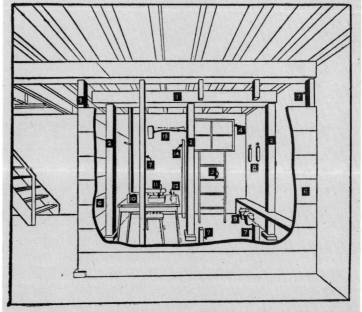

The air raid shelter recommended for cellars of one and two-family dwellings by the Bomb Shelter Committee of the New York City Civil Defense Organization.

Key to above diagram:

(1) 6"x6" or larger girder placed under present floor beams to reduce span.

(2) 6"x6" wood posts or 4" diameter pipe columns, under girder about four feet apart.

(3) 6"x6" wood post or 4" diameter pipe column under present girder.

(4) Window for a second exit to outside. Should be covered on inside with heavy one-half inch mesh screening. A sandbag or heavy timber enclosure in the form of a well to the top of the window, should be placed outside of the window. The window should be fastened open at the air raid warning signal. The window should be at least 24"x24" in size.

(5) Ladder to window.

(6) Wood concrete or sandbag enclosure at least six feet high.

(7) 2"x4" wood studs, 24" apart for wood enclosure.

(8) Fire extinguishers.

(9) Pails of water.

(10) Battery operated radio.

(11) First-aid kit.

(12) Battery lantern.

(13) Axe.

(14) Crowbar.

The Bomb Shelter Committee said the shelter should be approximately eight feet by ten feet in size. The Committee said that an empty, concrete enclosed coal bin may be used as a shelter with the safety measures shown in the diagram.

The swept-back ducktail

Poodles and Apaches

One of the most personal fads of the
'50s was the odd hairdo. Girls appeared in the
skull-hugging poodle and the pretty ones
got away with it. But boys who went for the swooping
ducktail or the starkly furrowed Apache
could find themselves in trouble:
in February 1957 a Massachusetts school
banned anyone with a ducktail.

The close-shaved Apache

Actresses (left to right) Denise Darcel, Peggy Ann Garner, Ann Sothern and Faye Emerson show off their curly poodle cuts in 1951.

147

Real George Is With It All the Way

Of all the fads that came and went in the '50s, perhaps the oddest was the disorientation of the English language. Styles in slang changed faster than the hemlines of Dior dresses, and words sometimes performed complete 180-degree turns in the course of the decade. Thus, "hot" in 1950 soon changed to "cool," "real gone" became "the most," what was "in" became "out," and soon "way, way out" was just about as "in" as one could get.

Adding to the confusion was the fact that different groups of people spoke their own particular slang. Jazz musicians conversed in one lingo, teenagers in another, hot rodders and space scientists in still others *(below)*, and Madison Avenue executives in something else again. But all groups shared one thing in common; nobody wanted to be labeled square *(opposite)*. For in a decade when everybody tried just as hard as possible to behave just like everyone else in his own circle (which meant, according to his friends, that he was either cool, hip, smooth, shoe, real George, tweedy, with it, tough or wild), the last place anyone wanted to be was out of it.

JAZZ AND BEBOP SLANG

CRAZY (*also "frantic," "the most"*) —wonderful, great; also a general response to anything anyone said, so that "What's new, Jack" would be answered by "Hey, crazy man."

DIG—to understand, appreciate, or even notice, as in "Dig that crazy mixed-up blonde."

CAT (*also "stud"*)—a person who dug; any man.

DOG—a song that did not make it.

GONE (*also "cool," "groovy," "far out," "the end"*)—the superlative of crazy.

FLIP—to become enthusiastic, as in "The cat really flipped over the chick."

HIP—aware; a cat who dug was hip.

HIPPY—any person who was so supercool and far out that he appeared to be asleep when he was digging something the most.

BREAD (*also "geets," "green," "M"*) —money.

MEAN (*also "tough," "terrible"*)—words that replaced "crazy" to signify the greatest.

AXE—any musical instrument, from a saxophone to a piano.

BLOW—to play an axe, as in "He blows mean piano."

CHICK (*sometimes "sis"*)—a girl. An unattractive chick was a "bear" and a fat chick was known as "heavy cream."

MONKEY—a music critic. (He sees no music, hears no music, digs no music.)

TEEN-AGE LINGO

COOL (*also "neat," "smooth," "casual"*) —worthy of approval; as a noun, it denoted poise or self-assurance.

HANG LOOSE (*also "negative perspiration"*)—no sweat, don't worry.

HAIRY—formidable, as in a hairy exam.

CLUTCH—to panic, or lose one's cool.

YO-YO (*also "square," "nerd," "turkey," "spastic," "blow-lunch," "nosebleed"*)—a dull person; an outsider.

BLAST-OFF—go away, get lost, drop dead (*also "DDT" for "drop dead twice"*).

DRAG—anything, or anybody, that was considered dreary.

WHEELS—a car.

PASSION PIT—a drive-in movie.

GROUNDED—unable to borrow the family wheels to take a hot date to the passion pit.

SARC—sarcastic; a sarc remark would be, "Wanna lose ten ugly pounds? Cut off your head."

HARDEEHARHAR—the sarc response to someone else's bad joke.

HOT ROD ARGOT

DRAG—a race from a standing start.

BOMB (*also "screamer," "stormer," "hack," "draggin' wagon"*)—a souped-up car, or hot rod.

RAKING (*also "dagoing"*)—lowering the front end of a car to give it a streamlined look.

CHOPPING—lowering the roof of a car to give it a chopped top.

SKINS—tires; if they were whitewalls, they were called "snowballs."

DUALS (*also "stacks," "pipes," "Hollywoods"*)—a special exhaust system.

NERF-BAR—the bumper.

SPOOKING—a sophisticated term for bombing around, or driving someplace simply for the sake of driving.

SPACE SCIENCE GOBBLEDEGOOK

BIRD—a rocket, missile, earth satellite or any other inanimate flying object.

BEAST—a large bird.

IVORY TOWER—a vertical test stand.

STOVEPIPE—a missile's outside shell.

ELEPHANT EAR—a thick plate that reinforced hatches on the stovepipe.

SNAKEBITE—an accident.

EGADS BUTTON—pushed to blow up a missile that strayed off course, and thus might cause snakebite.

SQUARES ARE OUT

There are a hundred different uses of the word square. . . . Prowling into the subject in search of examples recently, the novelist Robert Sylvester heard these definitions from Manhattan to Montauk: "A square is someone who smokes without taking the band off his cigar; has luminous signs on his car bumpers . . . wears a pocket handkerchief with his initials showing . . . pays strict attention to all non-tipping signs; carries a portable radio to the ball game so he can follow the scores elsewhere; has trouble working the slots in the Automat; bothers to read the inscriptions on the photos of celebrities in restaurants; puts vermouth in a martini; and wears his hat brim a little wider than ours."

. . . Along Broadway, where the language acquires refinements—something like piling strawberries on the cheesecake at Lindy's—the squarest kind of square is called a cube. A cube is so square, they say, he can block his own hat. Another phrase for a real square is "way in," the opposite of someone real hip or "far out." Youngsters say: "He's a - - -," and finish the sentence by placing the index fingers together and drawing a square in the air. Another, somewhat sneakier way of calling someone a square in his presence is to describe him as an "L 7." By putting the letter and number like this—L 7—a crude square is formed.

Only the other day (jazz guitarist) Eddie Condon, asked about squares today, replied: "I don't use the word myself and never hear musicians who are professionals use it. I'd say that musicians who call people squares are squares." That squares the circle.

HERBERT MITGANG IN *THE NEW YORK TIMES MAGAZINE*

FINALIZE IS IN

My Madison Avenue etymologist, who has been assigned the task of keeping abreast of the English language employed by the ad people, blew in the other day, his brief case bulging. "Let's pressure-cook it," he announced cheerfully.

He had me there. "I'm soft as a grape," I murmured. "Throw me the spellout."

"Okay, crowd in," he said, pulling out a document from his brief case. "See what you can make of this letter that went out from an agency the other day: 'You are absolutely right about how it figures—TV is pricing itself right out of the market. What frosts us is that . . . the only way you can go home with your skin on is to buy the stuff packaged. . . .' "

I took a deep breath. "It doesn't quite jell with me," I said. "When you glim the over-all picture, you must realize there are certain rock-bottom slants which have to be considered before the final wrap-up," I paused. "How am I doing?"

"Just fair. You are still too definite. . . . You got to housebreak it for the top brass."

"Housebreak it? That's a new one. How do you housebreak an idea?"

"You kick it around. You take a reading of the general situation to be sure that the whole picture hasn't changed. You gather the gang and spit-ball until the wrinkles are ironed out. You mother-hen it. You talk off the top of your head and the bottom of your pants. In short, you finalize it. By that time it's so thoroughly housebroken its mother wouldn't recognize it."

JOHN CROSBY IN THE *NEW YORK HERALD TRIBUNE*

Baton-twirling contest at Soldier Field, Chicago, 1957.

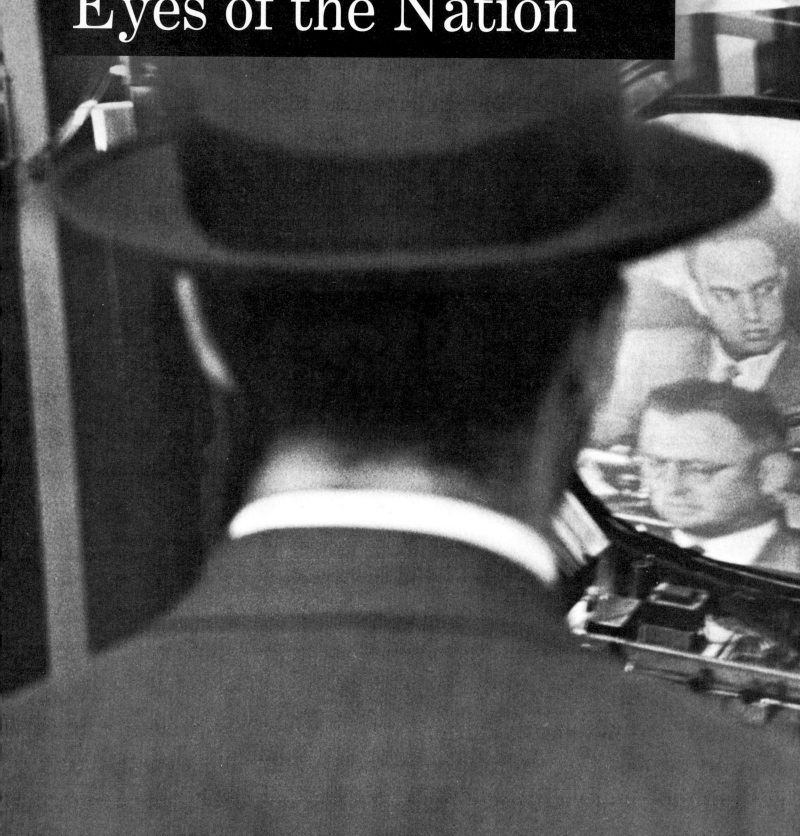

The Political Circus

Sincerity is the quality that comes through on television. RICHARD M. NIXON, 1955

Does it sort out the charlatan from the statesman? Are we quite sure that Father Coughlin and Huey Long wouldn't have been bigger with the help of television? EDWARD R. MURROW, 1952

The most enthralling television performer of the '50s was not Milton Berle or Dick Clark, but that master of bravado and showmanship, the American politician. To a vast home audience the close-up of Congressional committees and political conventions provided by television proved as fascinating as firsthand observation of politics had been in the era of the town meeting. And when the real spectaculars were on view, schools closed, department-store sales dropped and movies played to vacant houses—until the theater owners got smart and piped the political extravaganzas onto their screens.

The first significant performance was a televised road show staged by Senator Estes Kefauver and his Special Committee to Investigate Organized Crime. Before it opened in Miami in May of 1950, Kefauver was just another obscure, though quietly ambitious, legislator known to few beyond his Tennessee constituency. But as the Crime Committee swung through six major cities, playing a deadly game of question-and-answer with a Runyonesque assortment of crooks and political favor peddlers, the rustic Senator acquired a following that, said TV critic John Crosby, "even Howdy Doody might envy." By the time the climax came in New York City,

Estes Kefauver had become perhaps the best-known American short of the President—whose office would be contested the following year.

Another shrewd politician turned the TV camera to good use 18 months later when G.O.P. Vice-Presidential nominee Richard M. Nixon, beset by charges that he had accepted improper campaign contributions, went on nationwide TV to throw himself at the mercy of the voters. Nixon's plea, though it never really dealt with the specific charges ("Pat and I have the satisfaction that every dime that we've got is honestly ours. I should say this—that Pat doesn't have a mink coat, but she does have a respectable Republican cloth coat..."), had such homely appeal that the voters welcomed him back aboard. Less than two years later, the kingmaking camera turned on one of its users and destroyed him, as Senator Joseph R. McCarthy bellowed his way to his own demise during a Senatorial investigation of charges and countercharges between him and the Secretary of the Army. Following this debacle, a television executive prophesied, "Perhaps television is going to change the one great American habit which none of us thought too much about—apathy."

A New York movie theater drops its regular Hollywood fare to pick up television's political spectacular, the Kefauver hearings.

Estes Kefauver and his dour-faced colleagues opened their New York City engagement at the drab Foley Square Federal Courthouse before some 20 million TV fans. But as Chief Counsel Rudolph Halley snapped questions at a fascinating parade of tight-lipped Mafia bosses, curvaceous molls and squirming pols *(following pages)*, the rave reviews for the show's entertainment value became mixed with some troubled queries about the effect TV might have on the whole process of government. In trying to answer one such question, Estes Kefauver himself gave unwitting proof *(bottom)* that the real answers might be a long time coming.

The opening session of the Senate Crime Investigating Committee was nothing less than a Hollywood thriller truly brought to life. The central characters could hardly have been cast to type more perfectly.

JACK GOULD, *NEW YORK TIMES* TELEVISION CRITIC

Here is the perfect combination of information and entertainment. Every bit of it is exciting stuff, and deserves all the presentation it is getting.

NEW YORK HERALD TRIBUNE

It was a great show. But was the televising of it legal? Was it ethical?

NEWSWEEK MAGAZINE

What about the rights of the witnesses who were haled before the committee and subjected to the heat, glare and public exposure of newsreels and television?

TELFORD TAYLOR, FORMER FCC OFFICIAL

Ridiculous! Nobody ever thought of me for President and certainly I never thought about it myself. I just want to be a United States Senator if I can, and if I can't be that I want to go back to Tennessee and be a country squire.

ESTES KEFAUVER

156

Committee members (from left): Charles Tobey of New Hampshire, Maryland's Herbert O'Conor, Kefauver and Counsel Halley.

Under the Big Top

When the Republicans and then the Democrats
convened at Chicago in the summer of 1952 to pick
Presidential candidates, the bulging eye
of television for the first time brought the delegates'
shrieking, foot-stomping, sign-waving antics
live to a national audience of fascinated TV watchers.

Americans had never seen anything quite like the 1952
Presidential nominating conventions. In 1948 television
had been too limited to show much of the action. But in
July 1952 the three major networks shipped 30 tons of
equipment and more than a thousand workers to Chicago's International Amphitheater; and when Republican National Chairman Guy Gabrielson whacked down
his opening gavel, 70 million Americans saw him do it.

Over the next three weeks of conventioneering, the
people had ringside seats to a first-class political war as
the G.O.P. fought to decide whether Dwight Eisenhower or Robert Taft would be its nominee; and the show
was every bit as good when the Democrats threw over a
succession of hopefuls while Adlai Stevenson wavered.

Televiewers saw the implied threat of patronage to
be given or withheld in every down beat of Tom Dewey's
stubby forefinger as he polled the New York delegation
for Eisenhower votes. And they saw him take a dam-
aging shot from Taft-backer Everett Dirksen, who
admonished: "Tom Dewey, we followed you before and
you took us down the road to defeat. And, don't do this
to us again." They watched with amusement as the camera caught G.O.P. Committeewoman Mrs. Charles
Howard slipping out of her shoes before stepping to the
microphone. They saw a dazed Kefauver face the real-
ization that he was out of the running. They heard the
eloquent, witty Stevenson introduce his running mate,
John Sparkman, as a prime piece of "political live-
stock." And they enjoyed a disarming moment of
frankness from an exhausted announcer battling his
way through a crowd after Ike's nomination: "We're
waiting for the General now. We don't know when he'll
come out. And frankly, I don't care any more."

A favorite with televiewers, CBS convention commentator Walter Cronkite drew criticism from his bosses, who said he "talked too much."

The G.O.P. Opens the Show

Ex-President Hoover castigates "dishonor in high places."

Pennsylvania Governor John Fine loudly demands a hearing.

Some young women for Eisenhower gather underneath ruffled parasols.

Tom Dewey supports Ike.

MacArthur denounces the Democrats.

California Governor Earl Warren's three daughters applaud a speech.

A delegate signals for a vote on the seating credentials.

Ike's floor manager Lodge grabs a bite.

Ohio's Bender and Dirksen of Illinois plump for Taft.

The Democrats Pick Their Man

F.D.R.'s widow is called "First Lady of the World."

Mavericks in the Texas delegation noisily protest the pro-Stevenson party line.

Vice-Presidential nominee Sparkman salutes the crowd.

A coonskin-capped Tennessean whoops for Kefauver.

Massachusetts' J. F. Kennedy

The convention cheers the rejected Vice-Presidential candidate Barkley.

South Carolina's Jimmy Byrnes hammers home a point.

Democratic war-horse Harry Truman fingers the new Presidential candidate, Adlai Stevenson.

Flanked by smiling wives, Ike and Vice-Presidential candidate Nixon kick off the campaign with a buoyant, hands-raised victory signal.

A Couple of Joes

For 36 days in 1954, a struggle for power raged in Washington. Technically, it was just a Senate subcommittee hearing on a dispute between Republican Senator Joseph R. McCarthy and the U.S. Army—but at stake was the integrity of the American political system. As the two sides set upon each other with charges and countercharges, 20 million Americans watched on television.

When, on the 30th day of the Army-McCarthy hearings, the end came for Senator Joseph R. McCarthy, he had just finished another harangue. His black-stubbled jowls were spread in the familiar wolfish grin as he awaited the usual tribute of applause. Instead the people—his people—who were jammed against the marble columns and crimson curtains of the Senate Caucus Room, applauded his enemy, another Joe named Welch. McCarthy seemed puzzled and suddenly alone. He held his palms up in bafflement and said: "What did I do?"

He had done nothing different, really, from what he had been doing for the past 1,700 days. During that time, the Wisconsin Republican turned Washington upside down. He had set up a retinue of civil-servant informants, exercised a virtual veto over State Department personnel and U.S. foreign policy, demoralized the Voice of America, driven from Washington four Senators who opposed his methods, charged two Presidents with treason, wrung sobs from the Secretary of the Army and added his name to the language as a symbol of persecution. All told, McCarthy had probably come as close to wrecking the U.S. political system as had any man in the previous century.

The era of McCarthyism began the night of February 9, 1950, in the old McLure Hotel in Wheeling, West Virginia, where the Senator had flown to address the local Republican Lincoln Day dinner. In the four and a half previous years—since the end of World War II —Communism had changed from ally to menace; and the United States, an essentially insular nation, had suddenly been thrust into leadership of a complex, contentious world. Nothing seemed to go right for the new leaders. Communists had taken over Czechoslovakia and Hungary and had conquered China; they had exploded an A-bomb and encircled West Berlin with a blockade. Americans were angry and bewildered. What had gone wrong? Had the U.S. been sold out? There were those who thought so. "Traitors in the high councils in our own government," said an ambitious California Congressman named Richard Nixon, "have made sure that the deck is stacked on the Soviet side."

The House Un-American Activities Committee began to seek out the traitors. To the astonishment of some Americans and the dismay of all, it found some. A number of government employees who were Communists or Communist sympathizers apparently had fed highly confidential information to the Russians. Several of them were convicted of various crimes in the aftermath of the committee hearings—notably a one-time State Department official named Alger Hiss. There were not many such cases. But there were enough to lend a semblance of reasonableness to the growing Red scare.

It was at this moment that Joseph McCarthy stepped forward, claiming he had the names of live Reds, busy undermining the government right now. Holding aloft a document, he told his West Virginia audience: "I have here in my hand a list of 205 names known to the Secretary of State as being members of the Communist Party and who nevertheless are still working and shaping the policy of the State Department." Next day, when he spoke in Denver, the 205 Communists had become 205 "security risks;" the day after, in Salt Lake City, the 205 security risks changed to "57 card-carrying Communists"; 10 days later in the Senate the 57 Communists became "81 cases."

The fact was that there were no names at all. What McCarthy held in his hand that night was a three-year-old letter from former Secretary of State James Byrnes; it informed a Congressman that permanent tenure for 205 unnamed State employees might be denied on various grounds, including drunkenness. Six months after the Wheeling speech, a hastily convened Senate subcommittee concluded that the Senator had perpetrated a "fraud and a hoax." But no one was listening; an anxious nation was launched on a four-year binge of hysteria and character assassination. Americans needed to lay blame and Joseph McCarthy had offered them some simple, understandable targets.

In a later speech McCarthy conjured up more frightening arithmetic: "We've been losing to international Communism at the rate of 100 million people a year." Then, ominously: "Perhaps we should examine the background of the men who have done the planning, and let the American people decide whether . . . we've lost because of stumbling, fumbling idiocy, or because they planned it that way."

Millions of Americans listened as McCarthy, under protection of Senatorial immunity, then began naming names. He called Secretary of State Dean Acheson "The Red Dean." He described Far East expert Owen Lattimore as the "top Russian espionage agent in the U.S." and charged that U.S. Ambassador to the U.N. Philip Jessup was "preaching the Communist Party line." Besides name-calling McCarthy quickly proved that he could break people. Millard Tydings, a conservative Maryland Democrat who had chaired the 1950 Senate subcommittee that branded McCarthy's Wheeling charges a "hoax," ran for reelection later that year. McCarthy was waiting. He had a composite photograph put together purporting to show Tydings talking amiably with former U.S. Communist chief Earl Browder, saturated Maryland with copies and was widely credited with defeating the Senator's bid for a sure fifth term. He also took the scalps of other Senators who got in his way, among them Senate Democratic floor leader Scott Lucas of Illinois, Ernest MacFarland of Arizona and William Benton and Raymond Baldwin of Connecticut. He accused the Voice of America of deliberately constructing two radio transmitters where they would be ineffective; M.I.T. and RCA experts later disproved McCarthy but by then one engineer who had been in-

volved had committed suicide. McCarthy encouraged fanatical anti-Communist government workers to leak confidential documents to him and grinned that he commanded a "Loyal American Underground."

This was McCarthyism, the exploitation of a nation's fears, a brutal attack on Americans with divergent views, and it became an overriding fact of American life. Although in four years McCarthy was unable to offer legal support for a single charge, nevertheless people were stampeded. "McCarthy may have something," said Massachusetts Congressman John F. Kennedy. Truman's Attorney General, J. Howard McGrath, in 1952 ordered six detention camps readied to incarcerate alleged spies and saboteurs.

To Republicans, who had been out of power for nearly 20 years, McCarthy seemed to be a godsend: The charges he was throwing at alleged Communists invariably wound up besmirching Democrats. In the Senate cloakroom, John Bricker, the 1944 G.O.P. Vice-Presidential candidate, said: "Joe, you're a dirty son of a bitch but there are times when you've got to have a son of a bitch around, and this is one of them." The usually high-minded Senator Robert Taft, his eye on the '52 Presidential nomination, told McCarthy: "If one case doesn't work, try another." McCarthy himself, suddenly propelled from backwoods nonentity to party luminary, was cynical about his new fame and power. To a woman who asked him at a March cocktail party "When did you discover Communism?" he gaily answered, "Why, about two and a half months ago." But he cherished every ounce of his new status. He had, in fact, been striving for it almost all his 41 years.

Joseph McCarthy was that classic American figure, the poor farm boy battling to escape the harsh, sterile dirt farm of his youth, determined to get his share of the American dream. As a youth Joe had tried to make it chicken farming, then tried being a chain-grocery manager. At 20 he quit, crammed four years of high school into one and got into Marquette University, where he made ends meet by jockeying a gas pump, playing poker and coaching boxing. He moved ahead, twisting and turning. At college he switched from engineering to law, in politics he ran for local office as a Democrat and lost, then switched to Republican and won, becoming a Wisconsin circuit court judge. After World War II he made it to the United States Senate.

McCarthy's first three years in the Senate marked him as simply another ambitious young legislator —somewhat prone to use the knee and the elbow, but always with a smile, a wisecrack, the friendly, open look of the American boy playing the get-ahead game, certain everyone understood he meant nothing personal. Joe wasn't mad at anybody, he was just going places. He briefly supported the interests of the sugar and soft drink industries and acquired the Washington nickname of "The Pepsi-Cola Kid," then served the housing interests and got himself called "Water Boy of the Real Estate Lobby." To please his German-American constituents he intruded into a Senate investigation of 43 Nazi SS men who had confessed to murdering captured GIs during the Battle of the Bulge and so helped muddy the proceedings of the "Malmédy Massacre" hearings that the murderers were spared. It kept him busy, but it didn't seem to be getting him anywhere.

Then, in Wheeling that February evening as the '50s began, Joe finally caught hold of a star and started his meteoric climb. Within a few months he was describing President Truman and Acheson as "the Pied Pipers of the Politburo," adding of the President: "The son of a bitch ought to be impeached." He called General George C. Marshall, Chief of the U.S. General Staff in World War II and later Secretary of State, "a man steeped in falsehood," and "an instrument of the Soviet conspiracy." This was going a bit far, and Dwight Eisenhower bristled with rage at the slur on his former commander. Nevertheless, in July of 1952, the same Republican Presidential convention that nominated Ike invited McCarthy to address the delegates; convention chairman Walter Hallanan hailed the Senator, who had been a rear-echelon leatherneck in World War II, as "Wiscon-

sin's Fighting Marine"; and Joe strode through the Chicago International Amphitheater, to be cheered as the band blared "From the Halls of Montezuma." Later, when Ike stumped Wisconsin, he dropped from his prepared speech a paragraph extolling Marshall.

Although in all this time only a handful of Republicans had ever taken on McCarthy (Senator Margaret Chase Smith had attacked him in 1950 with the words: "I do not want to see the Republican Party ride to political victory on the Four Horsemen of Calumny—fear, ignorance, bigotry and smear"), many Republican and independent anti-McCarthyites believed in 1952 that only the G.O.P. could end his career. "McCarthyism would disappear overnight if Eisenhower were elected," predicted the *Washington Post*. And indeed the day after Ike's victory, McCarthy said, "Now it will be unnecessary for me to conduct a one-man campaign to expose Communists." Senator Taft commented: "We've got McCarthy where he can't do any harm." But in a few weeks the bad boy was back, doing business at the same stand, this time taking on not only Communists and Democrats, but the G.O.P. itself.

To Eisenhower's astonishment and anger, Joe charged the Administration with sending "perfumed notes" to friendly powers who were profiting from "blood trade" with Red China. He threatened to investigate the CIA. He fought Ike's nomination of Charles Bohlen as Ambassador to Moscow, claiming that the State Department's personnel chief, Scott McLeod, had not cleared Bohlen. (This incident disclosed an agreement by incoming Secretary of State John Foster Dulles to put McCarthy's friend McLeod in charge of hiring and firing. Dulles cleared all appointments with McLeod, who cleared them with McCarthy.) The Senator finally let the Bohlen appointment through, but only on the understanding that the Administration would make no further objectionable appointments.

By now Joseph McCarthy seemed to be the second most powerful man in the country. "The Senate," said the *Christian Science Monitor*, "is afraid of him." So, apparently, was everyone else. One day in 1953 a U.S. diplomat just back from abroad was handed a note by a State Department colleague: "Let's get out of here. This place is wired." They walked and the Washington official said: "You just don't know what's happened here. People don't talk at staff meetings any more. They've discovered that an opinion which is nonconformist is reported." Even Eisenhower was reluctant to throw down any challenge. Privately Ike described McCarthy as "a lawless man." But when Ike's advisers pleaded that the President strike down this apparently ungovernable menace, Ike declined. "I just will not," he said. "I refuse to get into the gutter with that guy."

There seemed no stopping McCarthy. He boasted: "McCarthyism is Americanism with its sleeve rolled." He gloried in being himself: the poor kid from the wrong side of the tracks who had fought his way up, who was going to teach the snobs a thing or two. "McCarthyism," wrote critic Peter Viereck, "is the revenge of the noses that for 20 years of fancy parties were pressed against the outside window pane." The Wisconsin Senator had tapped into one of the universal, recurring themes in American life: the antagonism between the uppitty, dudish, big-city smart alecks and the rough and ready, independent, true-blue Americans from the backwoods. "It is not the less fortunate . . . who have been selling this nation out," he cried, "but rather those who have had all the benefits—the finest homes, the finest college educations, and the finest jobs in government. The bright young men who are born with silver spoons in their mouths are the worst."

As 1954 began, McCarthy took on the biggest game of all. He amended his slam at the Democrats, "Twenty years of treason," and charged "Twenty-one years of treason." The meaning was amply clear. A few months later, when a *New York Herald Tribune* reporter attempted to question Ike about McCarthy, the President "clenched his hands together and . . . declining to talk, and nearly speechless with emotion, . . . strode from the room. His eyes appeared moist." As of that moment, the Senator seemed to have the whole country in his pocket.

But blinded by his success, he had already begun to overreach. In October 1953 he had launched an investigation of the U.S. Army, the pillar of order, and the heart of Ike's heart. The subject was supposed subversion at the Fort Monmouth Army Signal Corps Center. In January 1954 he went even further, questioning the routine promotion at Camp Kilmer of a leftish captain, Irving Peress. McCarthy inflamed the country with charges of "Communist coddling." He savaged Kilmer's commander, General Ralph Zwicker, a World War II combat hero: "You are a disgrace to the uniform. You're not fit to be an officer. You're ignorant." He bulldozed Army Secretary Robert Stevens, a well-bred, Yale-educated industrialist who tried fitfully to protect his men but ended in abject surrender, even offering McCarthy and his staff the use of his personal membership in New York's posh Merchant's Club (the bills to be sent to Stevens). Hounded and exhausted, the Army Secretary, sobbing over the telephone, offered to resign.

The confrontation finally came to a head when the Army drafted one of McCarthy's staff, a handsome young fellow named G. David Schine who pretended to a profound knowledge of Communism. Schine had been taken onto Joe's staff at the insistence of McCarthy's counsel and brain-truster, Roy Cohn, one of the most lordly 27-year-olds since Alexander of Macedon. Cohn drove the Army to distraction trying to wangle a commission for his crony. He phoned Stevens and Army Counsel John Adams innumerable times to argue for Schine. Some days he threatened to "wreck the Army."

And now, at last, even Ike had apparently had enough of McCarthyism; in any event he allowed his staff to move. On January 21, 1954, chief Presidential aide Sherman Adams secretly instructed the Army to prepare a brief to prove that McCarthy and Cohn were trying to blackmail it into commissioning Schine by threatening further investigations if it did not. In March the Army made the charges public. McCarthy countercharged that the Army was using David Schine as a hostage, in order to inhibit his investigation of the military.

On April 22, as a battery of TV cameras zeroed in on the Caucus Room *(right)*, a Senate subcommitee chaired by Republican Karl Mundt began to probe the conflicting charges. Superficially the hearings seemed to be a typical McCarthy performance. The Wisconsin Senator devastated the Army Secretary on the witness stand, threw the meetings into confusion with repeated cries of "point of order" and on the whole seemed to be well ahead in the early scoring. But there was one difference. Now and then, as some 20 million televiewers listened with fascination to the exchanges of dialogue, an elderly, bow-tied gentleman who had been appointed special counsel for the Army would intervene gently, softly, quizzically. Slowly he began to emerge as a major figure in the hearings.

Unlike Joseph McCarthy, Joseph Welch did little to bring to mind the hardscrabble Midwest farm country where he was born and raised. At age 24 Welch had entered Harvard on a law school scholarship and he had stayed on in Massachusetts, becoming, as converts often do, more Boston than the Bostonians. At 63, Welch had all the attributes of the Beacon Hill brahmin—the large, old-fashioned bow ties, the rumpled coat, the colonial house, the assured, lifelong Republicanism, the partnership in the old, conservative law firm of Hale & Dorr, where alone of 19 partners, he worked at an old-fashioned stand-up desk.

Joe Welch had as obviously made his arrangements with society as Joe McCarthy had not, and Welch fought with all the knowledge, guile and toughness that had made that society to begin with and that had preserved it ever since. The duel between the two men quickly captured national attention. Welch, his manner

PRIVATE G. DAVID SCHINE

soft, his mind sharp, cut deftly at McCarthy's case; McCarthy roared and raged back. On the 30th day, the climax occurred, unexpectedly and dramatically.

Welch was questioning Cohn, needling him, asking why Cohn had not stormed at the Army to proclaim that Communists were flourishing at Fort Monmouth. Cohn, trying to answer, began stumbling, sounding indeed as witnesses had sounded in front of McCarthy—seeking words, pleading bad memory: "I don't remember...I don't know whether..." As Welch bore in, McCarthy, squirming as his side took the sort of punishment he usually enjoyed administering, interrupted. It was fairly well known that when Welch became the special Army counsel, he had considered using as an aide a young lawyer named Fred Fisher from his own firm. On learning, however, that Fisher had once been a member of the National Lawyer's Guild, a pro-Communist organization, Welch, to avoid making an issue of him had sent Fisher home. Now the furious McCarthy lost all discretion and lunged after Fisher before the subcommittee and the TV audience. He went on and on, reviling Fisher for no reason relevant to the hearings.

At last Welch had had enough; suddenly he turned on McCarthy. His honest, emotional indignation was in sharp contrast with his usual calm demeanor, and even more so with McCarthy's brutality, coarseness and irresponsibility. This contrast was stamped indelibly on the mind of the nation. When Welch had finished speaking, he walked away in the corridor, as though McCarthy were unclean. The next day, front pages all over the nation showed the two Joes: McCarthy smiling as he savaged Fred Fisher, and Welch weeping quietly, as if for his country.

A seven-man Senate subcommittee (left side of table) hears the dispute between the U.S. Army and Joe McCarthy (far end of table).

Welch speaks out.

WELCH: *Until this moment, Senator, I think I never really gauged your cruelty or your recklessness. Fred Fisher is starting what looks to be a brilliant career with us. Little did I dream you could be so reckless and so cruel as to do an injury to that lad. I fear he shall always bear a scar needlessly inflicted by you. . . . Let us not assassinate this lad further, Senator. You have done enough. Have you no sense of decency, sir, at long last? Have you left no sense of decency?*

Cohn looks anxiously at a silent McCarthy.

Music

A rock singer wrestles with his guitar.

From Pop to Rock

Ladies and gentlemen, I'd like to do a song now, that tells a little story,
that really makes a lot of sense—"Awopbopaloobop—alopbamboom!
Tutti-frutti! All rootie! Tutti-frutti! All rootie!"

ELVIS PRESLEY, 1956

Ever since the middle of the 1940s, the average age of record-buyers had been dropping fast. But in the early years of the '50s that average age had not yet skidded into the teens; the typical record-store customer was in his early twenties, a so-called young adult. To suit his taste, most popular music was still bland and "sophisticated." The top male stars of the period were smooth crooners like Eddie Fisher ("O My Pa-Pa"), Harry Belafonte ("Jamaica Farewell") and Perry Como, who ambled with antiseptic amiability through his Saturday evening TV show murmuring nice-guy ballads. Females were usually sleek jazz stylists like Peggy Lee, Lena Horne and Julie London. Everything about these stars was grown-up and polished, and the songs of the period were lushly orchestrated hunks of pure romance. About the wildest thing happening was Rosemary Clooney performing bouncy little novelty tunes.

But while the grownups were dozing to Mario Lanza and Tony Bennett, the age level of record purchasers kept plummeting until 1958, when teenagers were buying 70 per cent of all records. Simultaneously the world of popular music was inundated by a wild new sound called rock and roll, a thundering mixture of country-western music with rhythm and blues. The performers who introduced the new sound struck most adults as being callow, pimply faced boys with ducktail haircuts and untrained voices, emitting mindless and frequently repulsive grunts. The rhythm of rock seemed overpowering and monotonous, the volume deafening and the movements made by performers scandalous. Even more scandalous were some of the lyrics: "Make me feel real loose, Like a long-necked goose. Oh, Baby, that's-a what I like." In fact, the very term "rock and roll," coined by New York disc jockey Alan Freed, was inspired by a raunchy old blues lyric, "My baby rocks me with a steady roll." Yet the new genre was clearly irresistible to the teen-age girls who now dominated the music market; they made national idols (and overnight millionaires) of adolescent guitar-thumpers and bought rock records in quantities beyond the wildest pop dreams of Dinah Shore and even Frank Sinatra. The genteel singers on TV's traditional pop showcase *Your Hit Parade* sounded like fools when they tried to warble "You Ain't Nothin' But a Hound Dog," and by mid-1957 the program went off the air, drowned by the teen-age tidal wave of rock and roll.

KAY STARR
Wheel of Fortune

PEGGY LEE
Fever

Rock and roll stars were almost all young men, belting
out their famous hits to the most avid rock fans—young girls. Singers like
the Everly Brothers were excellent musicians, but the likes
of Fabian, who could scarcely hold a note, were idolized as typical teens.

FRANKIE AVALON
Venus

FABIAN
Turn Me Loose

LITTLE ANTHONY
Tears on My Pillow

BOBBY DARIN
Mack the Knife

EVERLY BROTHERS
All I Have To Do Is Dream

LLOYD PRICE
Personality

RICKY NELSON
Poor Little Fool

A Swinging Prophet

The man who turned rock and roll into a national teenage religion was a 21-year-old Memphis truck driver named Elvis Presley. And he did it, of all places, on the Dorsey brothers' TV show, one of the bastions of four-sided pop music. The moment Elvis stepped to the mike and set his electric guitar to bellowing with a series of full-armed whacks, it was obvious that he was different. His voice shouted and trembled as though it, too, were electrified; and his way of moving was nothing short of orgiastic. So freely did Elvis bump, grind and shimmy his way through the show that Ed Sullivan pronounced him "unfit for a family audience."

The young girls in virtually every American family pronounced otherwise. Presley's first LP record *(right)* leaped to the top of *Billboard* magazine's weekly ratings; his singles ("Heartbreak Hotel," "Don't Be Cruel" and "Love Me Tender") each sold over a million copies. Finally, in late 1956, Ed Sullivan took a large bite of crow and hired Elvis for three appearances at an unprecedented $50,000, while still insisting that Presley be permitted on camera only from the waist up.

Although Elvis turned rock into an opiate for teenagers, he did not invent the form—a blending of the music of white back-country balladeers with black rhythm-and-blues that had been evolving gradually as social strictures loosened and each became more aware of the other. Then in 1954 the Chords hit it big when they wrote "Sh-Boom," and in 1955 Bill Haley and his all-white Comets scored with "Rock Around the Clock." But somehow Haley, et al., lacked the sex appeal to capture the youth market.

Enter, with a crash, Elvis Presley, followed by imitators who wiggled, wailed and cashed in handsomely but never truly threatened the prophet himself. By 1960 Elvis alone had sold $120 million worth of records, sheet music, movie tickets and merchandise; the T-shirt and tight dungarees he had worn as a poor kid in Memphis had given way to $10,000 gold lamé suits; and the truck he had driven for a living had been replaced by a fleet of gleaming pastel Cadillacs.

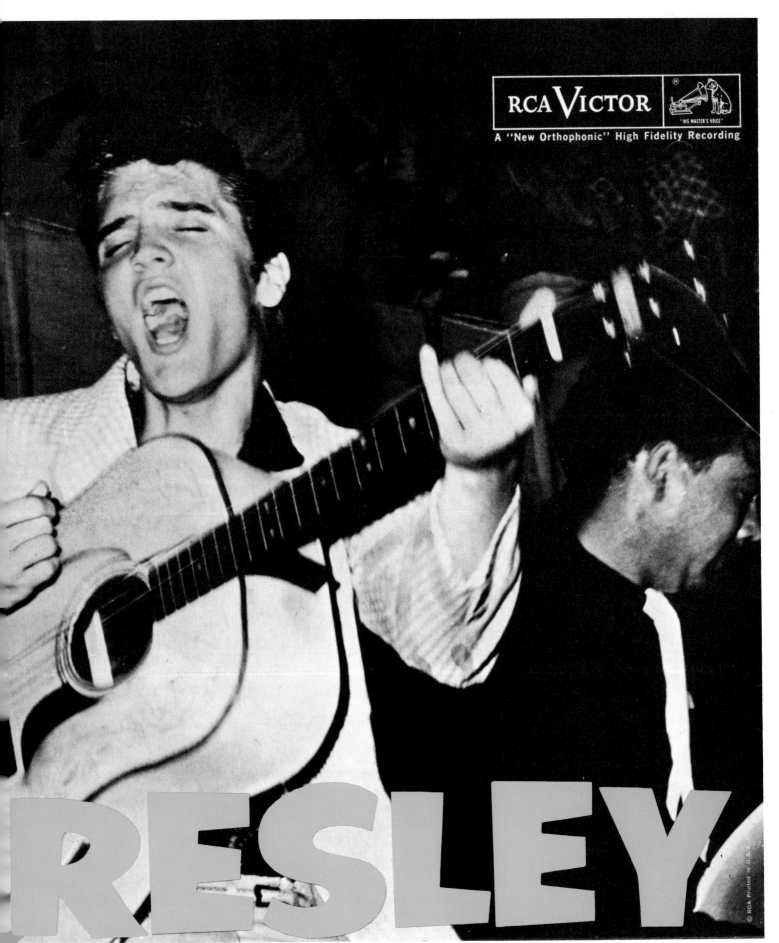

RCA VICTOR
A "New Orthophonic" High Fidelity Recording

"HIS MASTER'S VOICE"

RESLEY

© RCA Printed in U.S.A.

Elvis manhandles a microphone in Las Vegas (left) and shouts from the cover of his first LP, which featured "Blue Suede Shoes."

At his telecast 29th birthday party Clark greets Sal Mineo. Others include, at far left, rock singers Darin, Avalon and Boone.

Entrepreneur of Bedlam

Along with creating prosperous heroes from a flock of young singers, rock spawned the inevitable entrepreneurs who found ways to make hefty middleman's profits from the new sound. The most visible of these middlemen were the disc jockeys, and their undisputed king was a well-scrubbed square in his mid-twenties named Dick Clark, master of ceremonies for an afternoon TV show called *American Bandstand*.

Playing to the astounding total of 20 million regular weekday viewers, Clark paraded a stream of top rock stars before his cameras. But these celebrities rarely sang live on the show; rather, with a record of one of their hits going full blast, they moved their lips in synchronization with the sound. This technique was absolutely necessary for many of the unschooled rock singers. Once, when Clark asked Fabian to sing live a few bars from "Mary Had a Little Lamb," Fabian had to rehearse dozens of times.

While presiding over the parade of singers, Clark established his own weekly ratings of hits that became a national pecking order for rock stars. And he threw open the floor of his sprawling TV studio to young fans so that they could come on and dance while the music thundered. This odd entertainment earned Clark some $500,000 a year, 50,000 fan letters a week and the fawning attention of would-be rock singers, whom he could make or break at will. Connie Francis, Fabian and Bobby Darin, to name just three, owed their success to Clark's patronage. So influential did Clark become that one record-company salesman remarked that if Clark played a record "once a day for a week on his show, we could count on a sale in the stores of at least two hundred and fifty thousand."

This influence also earned Clark an investigation from the House of Representatives to see whether his rating of records and hopeful singers represented impartial judgments of merit. The probe cleared Clark of bribe-taking but did establish that the *Bandstand* emcee's financial interests were not harmed by the fact that he owned a record-pressing plant, a music publishing company, and a talent management firm.

Through all the hubbub, Clark remained the bland, short-haired square whose mission was to champion the cause of rock and roll: "What I'm trying to defend," he once wrote, "is my right and your right to go to a church of our choice, or buy the record of our choice." Typical of his boostership and sweetness-

DICK CLARK, *BANDSTAND* EMCEE

and-light approach was the system he devised for rating new releases; though his scale ran from zero to 100, he never rated a tune below 35 or over 98, "on the theory that no record is completely good or completely bad."

Teen-age fans adored this square peg who fitted so smoothly into their world. They lined up in regiments to get into his show so that they could rock and roll before his cameras—a fling performed so appealingly by some that they became bona fide celebrities in their own right. Most famous of the fans-turned-dancers was a winsome little blonde named Justine Corelli, who received hundreds of fan letters each week. Her sometime partner, Kenny Rossi, a 14-year-old "regular" in 1958, had 301 fan clubs.

One elderly viewer wrote Clark: "Please, Dick, as a special favor to an old farm woman, I would like to see Tony in another spotlight dance. Please do this, as Tony reminds me of someone I loved long, long ago and lost by death." So real did the electronic life of *Bandstand* become to viewers and participants that when a reporter asked dancing regular Mary Ann Cuff her plans for the future, she replied, "We *Bandstand* kids have a crazy dream. It's a baby idea. Maybe I better not say." "Oh, tell her," someone urged. "Well," Mary Ann confided, "What it is we all want is to get married and live on the same street in new houses. We'll call it Bandstand Ave."

1950

1 GOODNIGHT IRENE
  The Weavers and Gordon Jenkins
2 IT ISN'T FAIR—Sammy Kaye
3 THIRD MAN THEME—Anton Karas
4 MULE TRAIN—Frankie Laine
5 MONA LISA—Nat "King" Cole
6 MUSIC! MUSIC! MUSIC!—Teresa Brewer
7 I WANNA BE LOVED—Andrews Sisters
8 IF I KNEW YOU WERE COMIN'
  I'D'VE BAKED A CAKE—Eileen Barton
9 I CAN DREAM CAN'T I—Andrews Sisters
10 THAT LUCKY OLD SUN—Frankie Laine

The Big Sellers

The chart shown here of the 10 top records
for each year traces the triumph of rock and roll over pop.
But the old style did not die out completely:
The No. 1 record for 1957 was Debbie Reynolds' "Tammy."

1951

1 TENNESSEE WALTZ—Patti Page
2 HOW HIGH THE MOON
  Les Paul and Mary Ford
3 TOO YOUNG—Nat "King" Cole
4 BE MY LOVE—Mario Lanza
5 BECAUSE OF YOU—Tony Bennett
6 ON TOP OF OLD SMOKY
  The Weavers and Gordon Jenkins
7 IF—Perry Como
8 SIN—Eddy Howard
9 COME ON-A MY HOUSE—Rosemary Clooney
10 MOCKIN' BIRD HILL—Patti Page

1954

1 LITTLE THINGS MEAN A LOT
  Kitty Kallen
2 HEY THERE—Rosemary Clooney
3 WANTED—Perry Como
4 YOUNG AT HEART—Frank Sinatra
5 SH-BOOM—The Crew Cuts
6 THREE COINS IN THE FOUNTAIN
  The Four Aces
7 LITTLE SHOEMAKER—The Gaylords
8 OH! MY PA-PA—Eddie Fisher
9 SECRET LOVE—Doris Day
10 HAPPY WANDERER—Frank Weir

1957

1 TAMMY—Debbie Reynolds
2 LOVE LETTERS IN THE SAND
  Pat Boone
3 IT'S NOT FOR ME TO SAY
  Johnny Mathis
4 YOUNG LOVE—Tab Hunter
5 CHANCES ARE—Johnny Mathis
6 LITTLE DARLIN'—The Diamonds
7 BYE BYE LOVE—The Everly Brothers
8 ALL SHOOK UP—Elvis Presley
9 SO RARE—Jimmy Dorsey
10 ROUND AND ROUND—Perry Como

1952

1 CRY—Johnnie Ray
2 BLUE TANGO
  Leroy Anderson
3 ANY TIME—Eddie Fisher
4 DELICADO—Percy Faith
5 KISS OF FIRE—Georgia Gibbs
6 WHEEL OF FORTUNE—Kay Starr
7 TELL ME WHY—The Four Aces
8 I'M YOURS—Don Cornell
9 HERE IN MY HEART—Al Martino
10 AUF WIEDERSEH'N, SWEETHEART
  Vera Lynn

1955

1 ROCK AROUND THE CLOCK
  Bill Haley and the Comets
2 BALLAD OF DAVY CROCKETT—Bill Hayes
3 CHERRY PINK AND
  APPLE BLOSSOM WHITE—Perez Prado
4 MELODY OF LOVE—Billy Vaughn
5 YELLOW ROSE OF TEXAS—Mitch Miller
6 AIN'T THAT A SHAME—Pat Boone
7 SINCERELY—The McGuire Sisters
8 UNCHAINED MELODY—Les Baxter
9 CRAZY OTTO RAG—Crazy Otto
10 MISTER SANDMAN—The Chordettes

1958

1 VOLARE (NEL BLU, DIPINTO DI BLU)
  Domenico Modugno
2 IT'S ALL IN THE GAME—Tommy Edwards
3 PATRICIA—Perez Prado
4 ALL I HAVE TO DO IS DREAM
  The Everly Brothers
5 BIRD DOG—The Everly Brothers
6 LITTLE STAR—The Elegants
7 WITCH DOCTOR—David Seville
8 TWILIGHT TIME—The Platters
9 TEQUILA—The Champs
10 AT THE HOP—Danny and The Juniors

1953

1 SONG FROM THE MOULIN ROUGE
  Percy Faith
2 TILL I WALTZ AGAIN WITH YOU
  Teresa Brewer
3 APRIL IN PORTUGAL—Lee Baxter
4 VAYA CON DIOS—Les Paul and Mary Ford
5 I'M WALKING BEHIND YOU—Eddie Fisher
6 I BELIEVE—Frankie Laine
7 YOU YOU YOU—The Ames Brothers
8 DOGGIE IN THE WINDOW—Patti Page
9 WHY DON'T YOU BELIEVE ME—Joni James
10 PRETEND—Nat "King" Cole

1956

1 DON'T BE CRUEL—Elvis Presley
2 GREAT PRETENDER—The Platters
3 MY PRAYER—The Platters
4 WAYWARD WIND—Gogi Grant
5 WHATEVER WILL BE, WILL BE
  Doris Day
6 HEARTBREAK HOTEL—Elvis Presley
7 LISBON ANTIGUA—Nelson Riddle
8 CANADIAN SUNSET—Hugo Winterhalter
9 MOONGLOW and THEME
  FROM "PICNIC"—Morris Stoloff
10 HONKY TONK—Bill Doggett

1959

1 MACK THE KNIFE—Bobby Darin
2 BATTLE OF NEW ORLEANS
  Johnny Horton
3 VENUS—Frankie Avalon
4 LONELY BOY—Paul Anka
5 THERE GOES MY BABY—The Drifters
6 PERSONALITY—Lloyd Price
7 THREE BELLS—The Browns
8 PUT YOUR HEAD ON MY SHOULDER
  Paul Anka
9 SLEEP WALK—Santo and Johnny
10 COME SOFTLY TO ME—The Fleetwoods

One of the few singers to survive the transition from pop to rock, Pat Boone smiles through a collar of gold records (million-plus sellers).

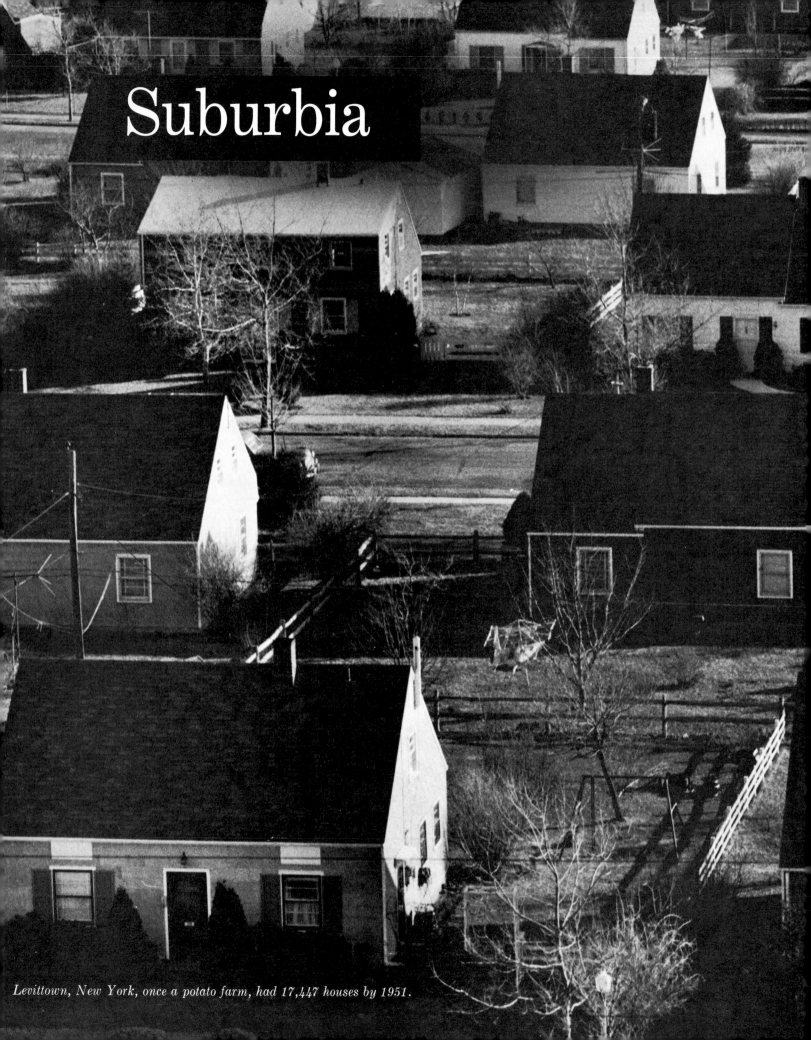

Suburbia

Levittown, New York, once a potato farm, had 17,447 houses by 1951.

The Battle of Babyville

The Moving Van is a symbol of more than our restlessness; it is the most conclusive possible evidence of our progress.　　　　LOUIS KRONENBERGER, *COMPANY MANNERS*, 1951

Some were rising executives; others only thought they were or pretended to be. Some were lawyers, dentists, steamfitters, teachers, stockbrokers, butchers, cops. In the '50s they moved by the millions to the suburbs, and the suburbs spread like patches of fungus to make room for them. There were houses for nearly everybody (1.396 million brand-new ones in 1950 alone), from eight-bedroom mansions on two-acre plots of ground ($62,000 in Greenwich, Connecticut) to little look-alike $6,000 boxes five feet apart in Daly City, California. And there were babies—so many that babyville became a synonym for suburbia.

Most of the new suburbanites said they had left the city in search of clean air, space, green stuff to look at and good schools. They usually got those things, but many had a more elusive goal that they did not discuss as freely: higher social status. Young husbands hoped for influential neighbors who might help them in their careers. Wives dreamed of entertainment in more sophisticated homes than they had known. To an extent these hopes came true. Status is self-conferrable. Cheerfully the new suburbs conferred it on themselves.

There were disadvantages. The men had weary commutes to work, either by faltering railroads (in 1955 nearly 40 percent of all New York, New Haven and Hartford trains were at least five minutes late) or crowded highways. They were faced with unaccustomed burdens such as lawnmowing. Taxes rose steeply to support the schools that were needed. Children could no longer be left with Grandma; she was usually out of reach, so when parents went out in the evenings, they had to employ a babysitter at 75 cents an hour.

The typical new suburb started from scratch on vacant land sold to subdividers, and its inhabitants hardly knew how to begin. Carefully they tended their grounds to win neighbors' approval and held backyard barbecues to cement chance acquiantanceships. They set up branches of national institutions—the Girl Scouts, the Little League, the P.T.A. and Cub Scouts—and sent their children to music and dancing classes. Cocktail parties grew into cocktail circuits and, though they were often derided, to be invited was a mark of social acceptance. By the decade's close, many a new suburb had built a convincing replica of Scarsdale—and already a few restless citizens were buying camping equipment to escape into the wilderness.

"I want to talk about something besides kids and illness!"

DRAWING BY CLAUDE. COPR. © 1956 THE NEW YORKER MAGAZINE, INC.

Commuters

	1950	1960
COMMUTER RAILROADS	46	30
RAIL COMMUTER PASSENGER RIDES *millions*	277	203
NEW YORK CITY AUTO COMMUTERS *thousands*	640 *est.*	866

Railroads cut back on their service. More and more commuters turned to highway transportation, as shown above in New York City.

This New York Central train on a January 1958 evening has seats for all. Many commuter trains had not, and passengers had to stand.

The 5:57 discharges commuters in Park Forest, Illinois. As commuter lines and facilities decreased, a national transit crisis loomed.

"My husband is the exact size of our picture window."

DRAWING BY PETER WYMA

Housing	1950	1960
U.S. HOMEOWNERS *millions*	23.6	32.8
NEW HOUSING UNITS STARTED *millions*	1.4	1.3
LAWN AND PORCH FURNITURE SALES *millions of dollars*	53.6	145.2

By 1960, with the peak postwar housing shortages already met, housing starts declined, but the sales of accessories, such as lawn and porch furniture, soared.

This development house was built in Sacramento at the peak of the boom. Lawn decorations like the flamingo above were standard items.

On a typically sunny day in Santa Barbara, California, the entire family gathers in the backyard for the ritual Sunday afternoon barbecue.

"Remember, Herbert, medium-burnt, not well-burnt."

DRAWING BY HENRY BOLTINOFF

The Barbecue	1950	1960
HOT DOG PRODUCTION *millions lbs.—est.*	750	1050
POTATO CHIP PRODUCTION *millions lbs.—est.*	320	532

The relatively minor increase in hot dog production reflected a turn to fancier, more substantial fare like hamburgers, steak, chicken, shish kebab and spare ribs.

A father herds his daughter and her fellow Brownies—plus one stray kid brother—to their regular Saturday ice-skating lesson.

"Am I glad to see you!!!"

© SATURDAY EVENING POST 1954

Children	1950	1960
CHILDREN 5-14 *millions*	24.3	35.5
LITTLE LEAGUES	776.0	5,700.0
GIRL SCOUTS AND BROWNIES *millions*	1.8	4.0
BICYCLE PRODUCTION *domestic and imported, millions*	2.0	3.8

Suburbia's raison d'être was good schools, community life and healthy surroundings. It all added up to kids.

Two den mothers join their Cub Scouts in the pledge of allegiance.

"Been a great bowling season, dear. Both the kids O.K.?"

Recreation	1950	1960
NATIONAL FOREST CAMPERS *millions*	1.5	6.6
BOWLING LANES *thousands*	52.5	108.0
OUTBOARD MOTORS IN USE *millions*	2.8	5.8

Suburbia was not only a new place to live, it was a new way to live, with more active sports, more simple fun.

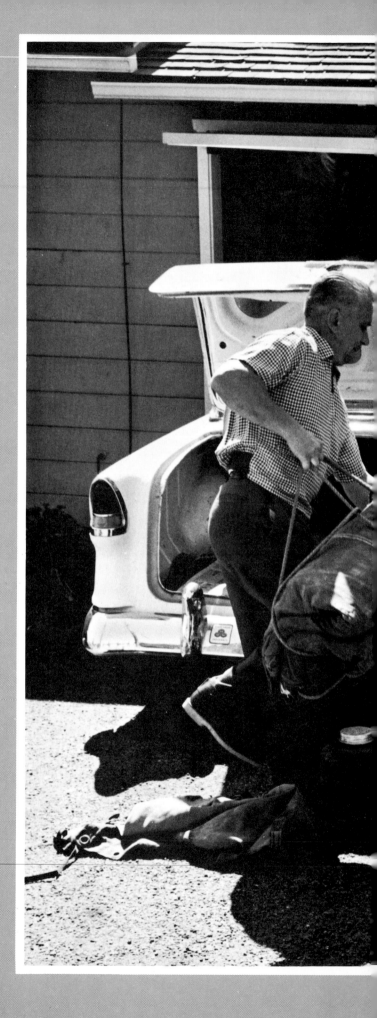

A family in Santa Barbara, California, packs for a camp-out. During the decade the number of recreation seekers more than doubled.

Picnickers from Ohio on the beach at Sarasota, Florida, 1940.

Drive-in movie, Moab, Utah, 1954.

Art lovers gather on the ramp of Manhattan's Guggenheim Museum, which opened in 1959.

The Cultural Muddle

There seems to be a Gresham's Law in cultural as well as monetary circulation: bad stuff drives out the good, since it is more easily understood and enjoyed.

DWIGHT MACDONALD IN DIOGENES, 1953

The prevailing mood is one of pessimism; in literary and intellectual circles there is much more talk of decadence than of renaissance. CECIL HEMLEY IN *COMMONWEAL*, 1954

Most critics, especially the highbrow kind *(above)*, deplored the mass culture of the '50s. And there was plenty to deplore. The preponderance of popular fare —Hollywood spectaculars, "horror" comics, hammering rock-and-roll music—had only one redeeming virtue: transience. Television was everyone's whipping boy; and in contemplating its fare, even middlebrow columnist Harriet Van Horne was crying cultural doom: "Our people are becoming less literate by the minute.... As old habits decline, such as reading books and thinking thoughts, TV will absorb their time. By the 21st Century our people doubtless will be squint-eyed, hunchbacked and fond of the dark."

There were real cultural dangers, no doubt of it. In this age of economic boom and mass media, culture, like toothpaste, was produced and consumed at a fearful rate; and this relentless pressure did tend to lower the quality of the product. Yet the situation was not so dismal as the pessimists claimed. For one thing, the much-abused media seemed quite responsible at times. In 1956, the National Broadcasting Company paid out $500,000 to present the premier of Laurence Olivier's film version of Shakespeare's *Richard III*. Fifty million

people tuned in, and about half of them stayed on through its entire three hours. *Life* magazine in 1952 regaled—or challenged—its several million readers by devoting a whole issue to the publication of Ernest Hemingway's new novel, *The Old Man and the Sea*.

There were other oases in the cultural wasteland. In painting, a group of innovators led by Jackson Pollock moved the capital of the art world from Paris to New York. Egghead humor, as purveyed by sharp-tongued satirists such as Mort Sahl, graduated from small clubs to big audiences on network variety shows. Paperback publishers propagated millions of copies of standard classics at prices low enough ($0.25 to $1.35) to attract cultural window-shoppers. Classical music was riding a spectacular wave of national interest. In mid-decade the country boasted some 200 symphony orchestras, up 80 per cent since 1940, and 2,500 towns offered concert series, an increase of 150 per cent in the same period. Music, in fact, went a long way toward proving that America's cultural oases might yet become bigger than the wasteland itself: in 1955 some 35 million people went to classical music performances—more than twice the year's attendance at major league baseball games.

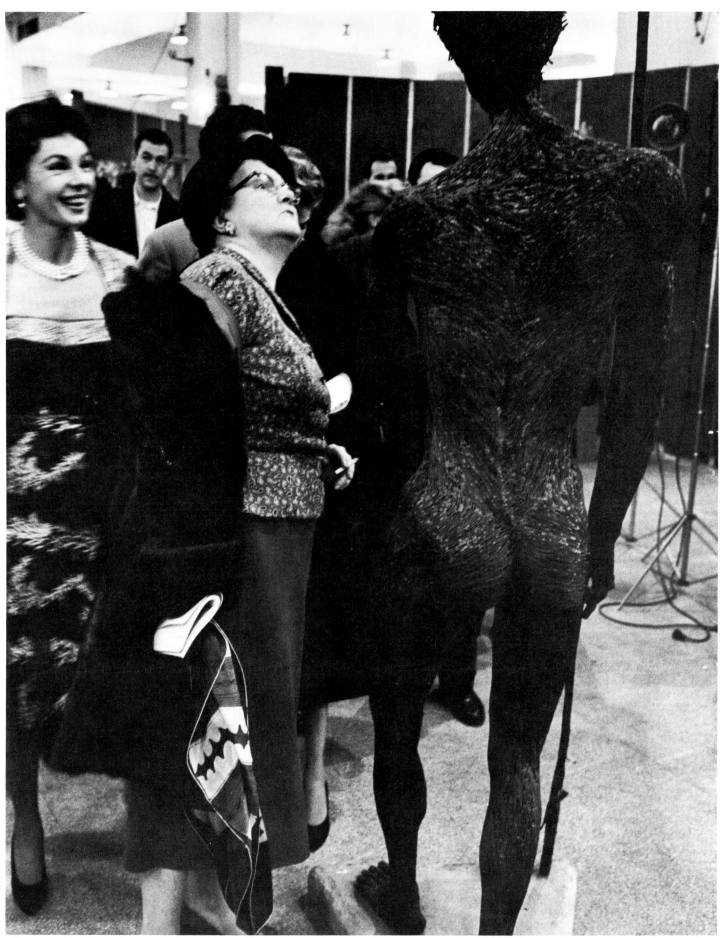

An earnest art lover peers quizzically at a welded wire statue by Kahlil Gibran, one of 1,500 works in a Madison Square Garden show.

Standing on a 17-foot canvas in his studio barn in the village of Springs, Long Island, Pollock drips and splatters enamel paint.

Jack the Dripper

In the mid-'40s, a handful of avant-garde art critics were caught up by the vast abstract canvases of a nonconformist named Jackson Pollock. The best known of the spontaneous "action" painters, Pollock dribbled paint on the canvas with a stick (left) or poured it directly from a can. From this his detractors (including "Time" magazine) dubbed him "Jack the Dripper" and described his art as "an explosion in a shingle mill." To those who vainly searched his work for a hidden message, Pollock had a word of advice: "It's just like a bed of flowers. You don't have to tear your hair out over what it means." By 1956 Pollock had won many converts, but in August of that year he lost his life in an automobile accident. Subsequently many of the same critics who made sport of him hailed him as "one of the greatest artists of our time." The final confirmation of his status came in 1960 —when a Jackson Pollock sold for $100,000.

On and Off the Rialto

Broadway took few risks during the '50s, banking heavily on big musicals of the kind that had set attendance records in the '40s. Typical of these was Meredith Willson's *The Music Man,* a corny family show about a con artist who tries to dupe a little Iowa town in 1912—but ends up as lovable as everyone else on the stage. Rodgers and Hammerstein, naturally, remained at the top of the field, scoring in 1951 with *The King and I,* in 1958 with *Flower Drum Song* and a year later with *Sound of Music.*

The biggest single hit of the decade was Lerner and Loewe's *My Fair Lady,* a musical adaptation of George Bernard Shaw's *Pygmalion.* Set in Edwardian England, the plot revolved around the attempt of Henry Higgins, a professor of phonetics (Rex Harrison), to teach Eliza Doolittle, a cockney girl (Julie Andrews), how to speak like a lady. Higgins succeeded, but Harrison very nearly flopped before the first curtain went up. Below he describes the struggles of composer Frederick Loewe and lyricist Alan Jay Lerner to convert him from a nonsinging dra-

matic actor into a musical comedy performer—a feat as formidable as the transformation of Eliza into a lady.

Two other successful variations on the Broadway theme were *Bye, Bye Birdie,* which spoofed a rock and roll singer resembling Elvis Presley, and *West Side Story.* Both shows modeled their heroes on America's newly rebellious youth, but *Birdie* was pure froth, while *West Side Story* was a powerful retelling of the tragic tale of *Romeo and Juliet* in terms of rival teen-age slum gangs.

The one new stage development of the decade was the growth of off-Broadway productions. The $250,000-plus cost of putting on a Broadway show and scalper prices up to $50 for orchestra seats triggered a migration downtown to low-cost houses in Greenwich Village. In 1954 *The Three-Penny Opera* opened there with an eyedropper budget of $9,000 and tickets scaled down as low as $1.75. Its dramatic excellence spurred an enormously successful rush of hole-in-the-wall productions, and, by 1956, off-Broadway was offering 68 shows to adventurous theatergoers.

Only once before had I ever sung on stage, and my reception indicated to me that I should never do a musical again. I spent an afternoon with Lerner and Loewe round a piano singing Gilbert and Sullivan, and so as to hide any embarrassment I might have, they sang along with me. If I remember correctly, it was dismal.

Anyway, once given all of my songs, it was suggested diplomatically that I go and have my voice—"placed" I think is the term. The first teacher I went to tried to train me in bel canto singing, which, of course, was ri-

diculous. After six lessons I chucked it, and when Lerner and Loewe returned to London I hadn't learned a thing. They then found me an instructor who was a tremendous believer in the use of the same mechanical methods for the spoken and sung word. Once again I began to sound like my natural, horrible self. I confess that if the conductor had not watched me constantly I'd have been lost. It's miraculous the way that he follows me, since, as I understand it, I'm supposed to be following him. As Higgins says, I am at best really just an ordinary man.

In the musical, "My Fair Lady," Rex Harrison teaches Julie Andrews to say her "h's": "In Hartford, Hereford and Hampshire. . . ."

The very model of a square but happy musician, Robert Preston directs a small-fry Iowa band in the 1957 hit "The Music Man."

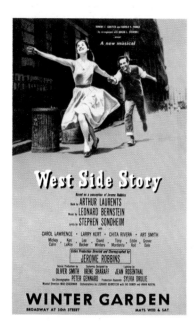

In "Bye, Bye Birdie," rock-and-roll star Conrad Birdie sings to a bevy of ecstatic teenagers.

In "West Side Story," a street-gang musical of "Romeo and Juliet," hoods with switchblades reenact the duel between Romeo and Tybalt.

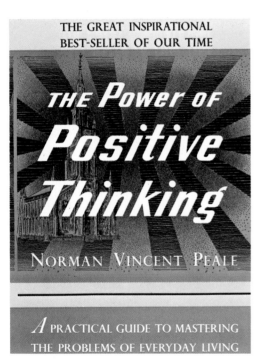

THE GREAT INSPIRATIONAL
BEST-SELLER OF OUR TIME

The Power of
Positive
Thinking

NORMAN VINCENT PEALE

A PRACTICAL GUIDE TO MASTERING
THE PROBLEMS OF EVERYDAY LIVING

The
EXURBANITES

BY A. C. SPECTORSKY

WITH DRAWINGS BY ROBERT OSBORN

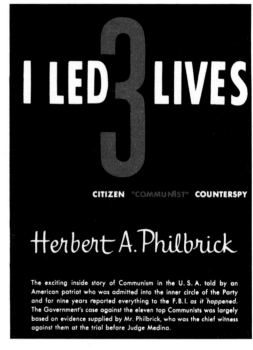

I LED 3 LIVES

CITIZEN "COMMUNIST" COUNTERSPY

Herbert A. Philbrick

The exciting inside story of Communism in the U. S. A. told by an
American patriot who was admitted into the inner circle of the Party
and for nine years reported everything to the F.B.I. *as it* happened.
The Government's case against the eleven top Communists was largely
based on evidence supplied by Mr. Philbrick, who was the chief witness
against them at the trial before Judge Medina.

THE STATUS
SEEKERS

AN EXPLORATION OF CLASS
BEHAVIOR IN AMERICA
AND THE HIDDEN BARRIERS
THAT AFFECT YOU,
YOUR COMMUNITY,
YOUR FUTURE

VANCE
PACKARD

AUTHOR OF
"THE HIDDEN PERSUADERS"

Jean Kerr
Co-author of KING OF HEARTS

PLEASE
DON'T EAT
THE
DAISIES

SIX MEN CROSS THE PACIFIC ON A RAFT

KON-
TIKI

BY THOR HEYERDAHL

A sampling of popular nonfiction reflects readers' taste for books that explore their own world. The subjects ranged from Thor Heyerdahl's

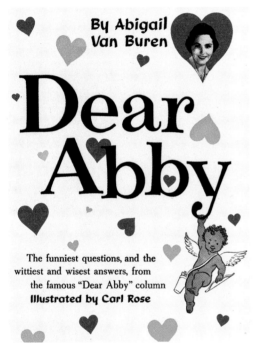

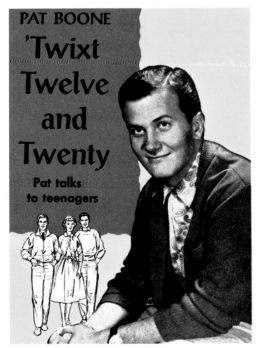

The Bestsellers

Below are the top-selling books of the '50s with the number of copies each book sold in the year it led.

Fiction

1950	THE CARDINAL	Henry Morton Robinson — 588,000
1951	FROM HERE TO ETERNITY	James Jones — 240,000
1952	THE SILVER CHALICE	Thomas B. Costain — 221,000
1953	THE ROBE	Lloyd C. Douglas — 188,000
1954	NOT AS A STRANGER	Morton Thompson — 178,000
1955	MARJORIE MORNINGSTAR	Herman Wouk — 191,000
1956	DON'T GO NEAR THE WATER	William Brinkley — 165,000
1957	BY LOVE POSSESSED	James Gould Cozzens — 217,000
1958	DOCTOR ZHIVAGO	Boris Pasternak — 500,000
1959	EXODUS	Leon Uris — 400,000

Nonfiction

1950	BETTY CROCKER'S PICTURE COOK BOOK	300,000
1951	LOOK YOUNGER, LIVE LONGER	Gayelord Hauser — 287,000
1952	THE HOLY BIBLE: *Revised Standard Version*	2,000,000
1953	THE HOLY BIBLE: *Revised Standard Version*	1,100,000
1954	THE HOLY BIBLE: *Revised Standard Version*	710,000
1955	GIFT FROM THE SEA	Anne Morrow Lindbergh — 430,000
1956	ARTHRITIS AND COMMON SENSE, *Revised Edition*	Dan Dale Alexander — 255,000
1957	KIDS SAY THE DARNDEST THINGS!	Art Linkletter — 175,000
1958	KIDS SAY THE DARNDEST THINGS!	Art Linkletter — 225,000
1959	'TWIXT TWELVE AND TWENTY	Pat Boone — 260,000

adventuresome "Kon-Tiki" to James Baldwin's bitter look at the reality of being black.

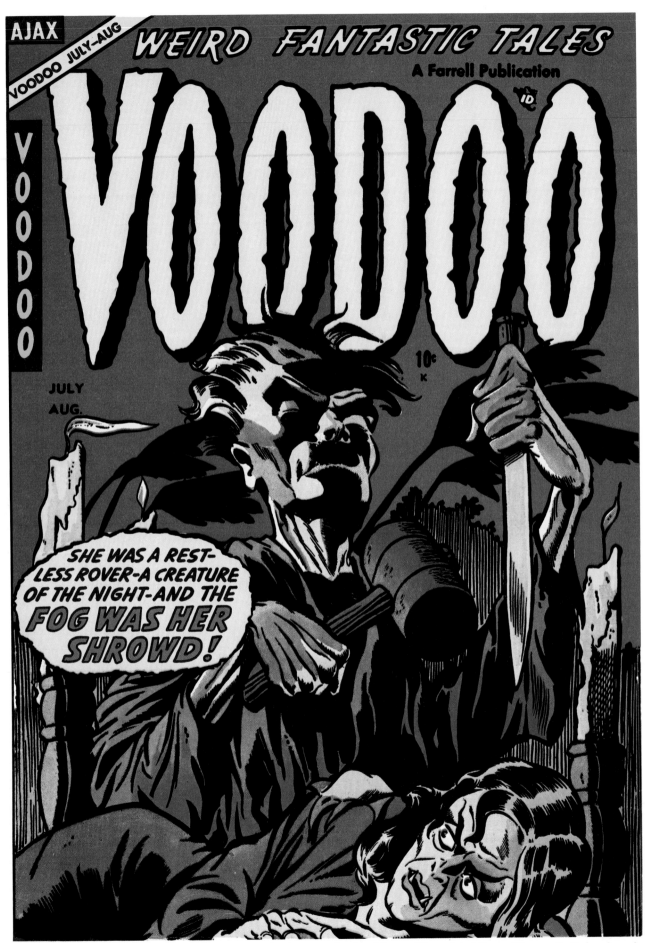

Besides serving up a brew of violence, horror books committed grisly spelling sins like putting a "w" in shroud.

No Laughing Matter

For years, the cheaper magazine racks had carried
a small spattering of horror comics but just before the decade opened, the market
unaccountably soared. By 1954, some 20 million 10-cent horror books
were being peddled every month (not counting the brisk second-hand market where used
comics went for one to three cents). Then, six states passed laws
regulating the sale of magazines to minors. As legal pressures mounted, publishers responded
with their own code of ethics and much of the dirty fun was over.

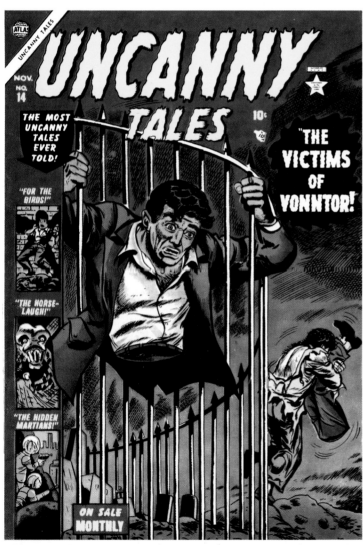

"Uncanny Tales" actually included some harmless science fiction.

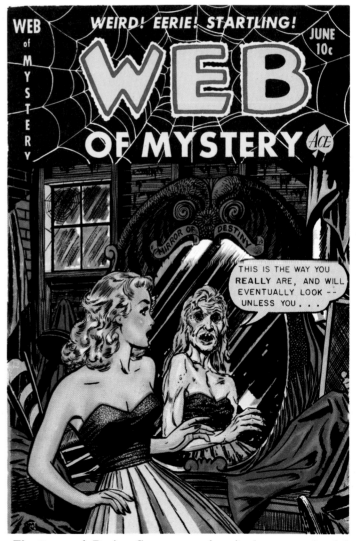

The theme of Dorian Gray was a favorite horror comic plot.

New magazines of the '50s (above) aimed at a special readership while the old general-audience favorite, "Collier's" (opposite), folded.

Cradle and Grave

*In the once stable world of legitimate magazine publishing, a half
dozen major new periodicals were born (one a virtual stillbirth), and one of
America's longtime favorites came to a sad end. Cowles Publications'
"Flair" offered a kind of jazzed-up culture at 50 cents a copy in a format that was
its own undoing: Accordion inserts, pages with artful cutouts and
a peekaboo cover burdened it with production costs that helped kill it after 12
issues. For the same price—50 cents—the young readers of Hugh
Hefner's fresh-as-paint "Playboy" got a foldout of a sexy pin-up Playmate (the
first one was Marilyn Monroe) and spoonfuls of "Playboy" philosophy; by
1960 its circulation was 1.1 million. Even younger readers in similar numbers
latched onto "Mad," a zany, truly funny comic that parodied the
passing scene—including even itself. "Jet" and "Sports Illustrated" both
began haltingly but picked up steam, "Jet" by dropping its girlie
image to become a black news and picture digest. Finally—and perhaps
ironically—a spruced-up catalogue of TV programs, "TV Guide," succeeded
beyond anyone's dreams (53 regional editions, 6.5 million circulation by
1959) while the ancient and honorable "Collier's," which for 38 years
had carried some of the nation's liveliest writing, was dying a slow, expensive
death before issuing its final edition (above) on January 4, 1957.*

Tittle-Tattle Tales

The decade's most sensational magazine was the scandal-chasing bimonthly, *Confidential*. Although its contents page boasted "No Fiction—All Fact," there were enough innuendos tucked between its lines, as in the issue sampled below, to keep its millions of readers pantingly happy and its lawyers in an ocean of hot water. Libel suits totaling seven million dollars were filed against it by screen star Robert Mitchum, millionairess Doris Duke, actress Maureen O'Hara and piano player Liberace. Cuba forbade its sale on the island after an exposé article on dictator Fulgencio Batista. The U.S. Post Office tried to bar it from the mails (over the objections of the American Civil Liberties Union). In 1957 the state of California charged *Confidential* with conspiracy to commit criminal libel and to disseminate obscene material, and this blow was very nearly mortal. Forced to stay away from Hollywood personalities and tone down stories, its readership plummeted to 400,000.

People in the know have heard and relayed scalp-raising yarns about Miss Bankhead's antics as a guest. There's the time she spent a week-end at a smart Long Island yacht basin and kept her wardrobe problem at a minimum by never once donning a stitch of clothes. Exhibiting her customary brass, Tallulah has told how she once was a guest in a London opium den. She brazenly recalls how, on another occasion, one of England's nobles who had entertained her for a week tried to snub her when they met at a later date. The poor fellow probably had his reasons for ducking, but Tallu refused to let him get by with it. In her voice that brays like an ocean liner's foghorn, she bellowed: "What's the mattah, dahling, don't you recognize me with my clothes on?"

Peron had been playing footsie with a politically powerful cabinet member who was also a notorious lecher. This official asked Peron if he could round up some party girls for a gay party at his ranch in "La Pampa" province. If Peron couldn't, Evita could. It was a natural. Remember, Evita had been an actress. She had contacts galore in the theatrical profession, and in the Latin American countries it is an accepted fact that actresses are also prostitutes.

Many famous actors and writers who belong to the third sex live at beaches such as Santa Monica, Venice and Ocean Park. You might be trampled to death at Santa Monica if you get in the way of bikini-wearing male Circes rushing to the section known as Muscle Beach.

Jack "Blubber" Astor, who gets his nickname because he looks as though he's smuggling Jello in his bulging dress suits, had and has such an interesting life he once hired a well-known publicity man (Ray Burgess) to keep his name out of the papers.

But Mario Lanza, though the fans don't know it, is living high off the hog and is one of the most exuberant stars of Hollywood, to put it mildly. At Metro ask any chorus girl who has worked in a Lanza musical in the days when the studio was trying to control his free-living personality. She'll tell you the word quickly zipped through the chorus line to beware of the fanny-patter and bust-pincher. CONFIDENTIAL, JANUARY 1954

The Mystical Bohemians

The only people for me are the mad ones, the ones who are mad to live, mad to talk, mad to be saved . . . the ones who never yawn or say a commonplace thing, but burn, burn, burn like fabulous yellow roman candles exploding like spiders across the stars.

JACK KEROUAC, ON THE ROAD

In the mid-'50s a new group of American-bred bohemians emerged, calling themselves the Beat Generation. "Beat," according to one theory, was a contraction of "beatitude"; the Beats felt that they had been blessed with mystical powers. But many of the new bohemians had fought in the Korean war and were disillusioned with the old American dream of prosperity and conformity; for them "Beat" simply meant "beaten down."

The beatniks, as they were soon known, were an easily recognizable breed. Originally a West Coast phenomenon, they first congregated in San Francisco and in Los Angeles' scruffy Venice West. The men favored beards but wore their hair short, and their clothing—usually khaki pants, a sweater and sandals—carefully avoided any hint of flamboyance. The girls wore black leotards and no lipstick, but so much eyeshadow that people joked about their "raccoon eyes."

They spoke their own argot, mostly picked up from jazz musicians and juvenile street gangs: "bread" for money and "like" as an all-purpose pause-word and qualifier. They experimented with marijuana, which they called "pot." Both sexes bundled up in flats they called "pads," furnished with no more than a guitar, a hot plate, a bare mattress and a few records and books. The records were usually of the most rarefied jazz (Miles Davis, Thelonius Monk) and the books were often about Zen, a Buddhist offshoot which taught that enlightenment could be achieved by abandoning rational, word-oriented thought. Although few Beats really understood Zen, it seemed to fit in with their longing for exotic experiences and instant inspiration.

To a nation acquiring a belated awareness of its own conformism, the rebellious life style of the new bohemians was both fascinating and repulsive. The mass media quickly exploited this ambivalence. The radio soap opera *Helen Trent* added a Beat character; Hollywood cranked out an exposé of Beat "orgies," and the big magazines treated them at best with condescension.

Amid the hubbub, Beat spokesmen carefully pointed out that they were not at all the dangerous revolutionaries that the "squares" imagined them to be. Novelist Jack Kerouac, a leading oracle of the movement, insisted: "We love everything—Bill Graham, the Big Ten, Rock and Roll, Zen, apple pie, Eisenhower—we dig it all. We're in the vanguard of the new religion."

A Beat folk singer strums a guitar in a dimly lit coffeehouse; Beats favored songs of protest—blues and Depression ballads.

Lawrence Ferlinghetti stands outside his San Francisco store.

The Beat Generation not only had a distinctive life style, it also produced its own literature. The literary center was San Francisco—critics spoke of the "San Francisco Renaissance"—and headquarters was a bookstore on Columbus Avenue called City Lights (after a Chaplin film). The store's owner was Lawrence Ferlinghetti, the eye in the center of the Beat storm. A poet himself, Ferlinghetti came to San Francisco in the early '50s, after working as a *Time* magazine mail boy, serving in the Navy and studying in Paris. One of his contributions to Beat literature was the reading and recording in 1957 of his poem "Tentative Description of a Dinner To Promote The Impeachment of President Eisenhower" with Cal Tjader on drums. He also became a book publisher, starting with his own poetry and then with editions of works by a poet named Gregory Corso, and by Allen Ginsberg, the minstrel of the Beats.

Copies of Ginsberg's poem "Howl" were seized by policemen in 1957 on grounds of obscenity (a local newspaper wrote: "San Francisco Cops Don't Want No Renaissance"). But a judge ruled that "Howl" had "redeeming social importance," and the trial brought notoriety to the Beat literary movement, which reached its peak during the next two years when Jack Kerouac's novel, *On The Road,* sold half a million copies. A saga of footloose bohemians who crisscrossed the country having visions and seducing girls, the book became a Bible to young people eager to Experience Life.

Beat customers browse idly through Ferlinghetti's City Lights Bookshop. The accommodating shop even held mail for itinerant authors.

Kenneth Rexroth

*The elder statesman of the Beats was Kenneth Rexroth, a former
popcorn machine operator, cowboy and cab driver whose readings of poetry and prose
on San Francisco's radio station KPFA gave a hefty boost to the local literary
ferment. Rexroth, who was in his fifties and himself both a poet and a painter, interested
his younger compatriots in Oriental culture through his
translations of Chinese and Japanese verse. With iconoclastic bravado he once announced,
"I write poetry to seduce women and overthrow the capitalist system."*

Gregory Corso

*The enfant terrible of Beatdom, Corso was a puckish, tousle-haired
product of New York's slums. At 16 he was arrested for attempting, with two other
friends, to take over New York City by means of a campaign of complex
robberies coordinated with walkie-talkies; for this he was arrested and put in Clinton
Prison for three years. After his release he educated himself at the
Harvard library, wrote poetry and, when interviewed, made inscrutable comments:
"Fried shoes. Like it means nothing. Don't shoot the warthog."*

Television

TV's top guns open fire: (from left) Cheyenne, of "Cheyenne"; Matt Dillon, "Gunsmoke";
Paladin, "Have Gun, Will Travel"; Flint McCullough, "Wagon Train"; Bret Maverick, "Maverick"; Vint Bonner, "Restless Gun."

The Electronic Opiate

Television is a triumph of equipment over people, and the minds that control it are so small that you could put them in the navel of a flea and still have enough room beside them for a network vice-president's heart.

FRED ALLEN

When General of the Army Dwight D. Eisenhower called a press conference in Abilene, Kansas, in June 1952 to announce his candidacy for President of the United States, a regiment of radio and newspapermen crushed around him to hear his words, while a small band of television cameras stood outside in the rain. To film the event for the home screen, cameraman Jesse Zousmer of CBS had to ram himself and his gear through the door. The rest of the newsmen howled that TV was usurping their special function and labeled the incident the Battle of Abilene.

When that battle was waged in 1952, the faces that generally dominated the nation's TV screens were vaudeville and radio comedians like Milton Berle *(opposite)*, who brought the guffaws of vaudeville into the living room. Many Americans believed that such fare was all the tube was good for. Intellectuals made a fetish of not owning an "idiot box"; preachers thundered that TV would corrupt the morals of the young. One movie tycoon, alarmed that theater attendance was dropping by the millions, said with more hope than foresight: "Video isn't able to hold onto the market it captures after the first six months. People soon get tired of staring at a plywood box every night."

But the fact was that television was in the process of dominating the communications industry. In 1950 there were TV sets in only 3.1 million U.S. homes. Halfway through the decade, the figure had jumped to 32 million. By the end of another year, Americans had spent $15.6 billion to buy sets and keep them repaired.

For all its eager acceptance by the people, TV continued to evoke much condemnation. It was called 'the boob tube" and "the light that failed." Some of the down-talking came from veteran performers who never managed to make the switch from radio to the new medium. One such was Fred Allen, who uttered the rueful words inscribed above. Other criticism came from newsman Edward R. Murrow, himself the decade's top TV commentator. "If television and radio are to be used for the entertainment of all of the people all of the time," he said, "we have come perilously close to discovering the real opiate of the people." Opiate it very nearly was. By 1959 the average U.S. family was sitting before the box some six hours a day, seven days a week.

Funnyman Milton Berle, known as "Mr. Television," kept millions glued to their TV sets on Tuesday nights for more than six years.

The indefatigable Lucy takes up ballet dancing—only to get herself trapped on the bar while her teacher looks on in helpless dismay.

Lucy's husband throws a fit.

Everybody Loved Lucy

Perhaps the zaniest and most
popular show of the decade was "I Love Lucy," a
spoof of married life starring
movie actress Lucille Ball and her Cuban-born
bandleader husband, Desi Arnaz. At
the end of its first six months of life, in 1952,
"Lucy" displaced Milton
Berle and Arthur Godfrey from top rating; less than
a year later its stars signed a contract for
eight million dollars, the biggest ever written in
TV. More people watched Lucy
mugging on Monday nights in January 1953 than
saw President Eisenhower's
inauguration in the same month, and the show
went on to lure an audience of 50 million viewers.

Lucy makes ready to throw a pie.

She dances with neighbor Ethel.

Situation Comedies

THE HONEYMOONERS

DOBIE GILLIS

OZZIE AND HARRIET

THE PHIL SILVERS SHOW

FATHER KNOWS BEST

LEAVE IT TO BEAVER

DECEMBER BRIDE

BURNS AND ALLEN SHOW

MR. PEEPERS

OUR MISS BROOKS

MAKE ROOM FOR DADDY

MAMA

MISS KILGALLEN   MR. ALLEN   MISS FRANCIS

Affable moderator John Daly grins at "What's My Line?" regulars and off-and-on guest panelist Steve Allen.

MR. CERF

The Career of "What's My Line?"

It was a pretty silly formula. A man or woman, called a challenger, would enter the studio and "sign in" on a blackboard. Then words would flash on the screen telling the audience what the challenger did for a living. The job was always far out—one man put sticks in popsicles, another sold church steeples, still another polished jelly beans. Then four panelists, using the old 20-Questions technique, would try to guess the occupation.

Despite this simple-minded format—or because of it —*What's My Line?* outlasted all other quiz shows at a time when quizzes were one of TV's staples. The particular appeal of *What's My Line?* lay in the regular members of the panel, a carefully mixed bag that, during the show's 17½-year run, changed hardly at all. There was quince-faced Dorothy Kilgallen, who asked the sharpest questions; cheerful and feminine Arlene Francis, who often guessed on impulse; and owlish Bennett Cerf, whose penchant for overripe puns (a cow that swallowed ink "mood indigo") camouflaged the fact that he was the shrewd chief of one of the nation's top publishing houses. They were joined by a fourth panelist, usually a well-known comedian. The comic was there for his quips; he was *not* supposed to guess the answer. The veterans took care of that, with an arsenal of questions *(below)* refined over the years to elicit a maximum of information with a minimum of effort.

A re you self-employed?

Do you deal in services?

Do you work for a profit-making organization?

Do people come to you? Men and women?

Are they happier when they leave?

Do you need a college education to do what you do?

Do you wear a uniform in doing this?

Is a product involved? Could I hold it in my hand?

Is it bigger than a bread box? Smaller than an elephant?

Ollie the Dragon chats with Kukla before moving in to administer a friendly bite to the nose of the gentle clown.

Affair of the Heart

While parents winced and educators muttered, the nation's first television generation gathered around the flickering blue tube when the sun went down to watch *The Lone Ranger* and *Hopalong Cassidy* beat the outlaws to the draw, to cheer *Lassie* and *Rin-Tin-Tin* as they rescued those in peril, to journey among the stars and the beep-blips of space in the gadget-filled ships of *Space Patrol* and *Captain Midnight*. Millions of small boys donned coonskin caps in emulation of *Disneyland's*

For reasons wholly incomprehensible to me this charming bit of satire . . . and fantasy . . . is . . . about to go off the air. Surely such an assassination, murther and mayhem cannot be permitted in this enlightened land of culture and sophistication. ADLAI STEVENSON

Davy Crockett and millions of treble voices joined Karen and Doreen in the *Mickey Mouse Club* theme song (M-i-c-k-e-y—M-o-u-s-e). Amidst all the noise one program charmed elders as much as it did children: Burr Tillstrom's gentle puppet show *Kukla, Fran and Ollie*. With no script and virtually no rehearsal, Kukla, the wise and bubbly clown, and sentimental, snaggle-toothed Oliver J. Dragon joined their real-live friend Fran Allison for a chat and a few songs. From time to time other Kuklapolitans were heard from, including Beulah Witch, Madame Ooglepuss, Fletcher Rabbit and Colonel Crackie (Tillstrom used 10 voices in the show, all of them his own). At its height *Kukla, Fran and Ollie* was seen by 10 million viewers on 57 stations and drew some 8,000 letters a week. But the all-important sponsors gradually began to drop away, unwilling to give the prime time of 7:00 p.m. to kids. Squeezed from half an hour down to 15 minutes in 1951, the show finally left the air entirely in 1957. When its demise was announced, NBC was bombarded with letters from devoted *Kukla, Fran and Ollie* fans, one of whom *(above)* was a former Presidential candidate.

"Dragnet" Sergeant Joe Friday and Officer Frank Smith question know-it-all landlady Daisy Wilkers about a 476 case—forgery.

Just the Cops, Ma'am

"It was Tuesday, January 11th. It was cool in Los Angeles. We were working the Day Watch out of Forgery Division. My partner's Frank Smith. The boss is Captain Welsh. My name's Friday."

Joe Friday was a TV cop. And for seven years (1952 to 1959) he was *the* cop for the millions of Americans who tuned in *Dragnet* weekly on NBC. Created by Jack Webb—who not only played Friday but directed the show and wrote many of the scripts—*Dragnet* was designed to show crime-busting as it really was. As the program's tagline made clear, its stories essentially were true: "Only the names were changed to protect the innocent." Each episode was based on actual cases taken from the files of the Los Angeles Police Department.

Unlike the shoot-'em-up orgies that had preceded it on radio and TV (*Gangbusters, Your FBI*), *Dragnet* dramatized the routine procedures police used to ferret out criminals. Sergeant Friday and his partner sent suspects' names and descriptions to "R & I" (Records and Identification) and sought their "M O's" (Modus Operandi). The show's set-piece attraction was the low-key questioning by the dour and laconic Sergeant Friday of an endless array of off-beat and equally laconic characters. Throughout the dialogue, Friday would remind them that "all I want is the facts. . . ." In the excerpt below, Friday and Frank Smith seek the facts about a forger who had been using the name of a dead actor to pass bad checks. The witness, Daisy Wilkers, is a devout movie fan who spotted the imposter and immediately called the police.

Audiences loved the show's deadpan realism; during the 1953-1954 season, *Dragnet* was second only to *I Love Lucy* as the most popular show on TV. The program's success bred a half-dozen imitators: CBS launched *Line-Up* in 1954 and ABC followed with *Naked City* in 1958. But none of them matched *Dragnet* in quality or—most importantly—ratings. When the final episode faded from the tube in September 1959, Joe Friday had scored his weekly triumph over the forces of evil, and *Dragnet* was still among the top TV favorites.

THE BIG BOUNCE

DAISY: You the policemen?

JOE: Yes ma'am. *(Shows I.D.)* My name's Friday. . . . This is Frank Smith.

FRANK: Hello.

DAISY: You certainly didn't hurry.

JOE: Traffic was heavy.

DAISY: Why didn't you use your siren?

JOE: Didn't want to scare him off.

DAISY: Too late to worry about that . . . left ten . . . fifteen minutes ago. . . . You might as well come inside.

JOE: Thanks.

DAISY: Suppose you'll want a full report. That's regular procedure, isn't it?

JOE: Go ahead, Miss Wilkers.

DAISY: Well . . . he came up to my door . . . Asked if I had a room for rent. I told him that was what the sign meant. He just laughed . . . like he thought I'd been making a joke. Didn't know I was serious . . . I said I wanted the first month in advance . . . I always insist on a *full month*. . . . Didn't bat an eye. . . . Just brought out his checkbook.

JOE: Now, did he ask if he could make it for a little extra?

DAISY: *(surprised)* How did you know?

JOE: Well, he's been around before.

DAISY: *(sharply)* If he's been around so long, why haven't you picked him up?

JOE: We're trying, ma'am. . . . That's when you called us?

DAISY: Course not. Didn't call you until I was sure the check was no good.

JOE: What made you sure it was phony?

DAISY: The way he signed it.

JOE: *(frowning)* What do you mean?

DAISY: Parker Allington. Trying to make me think he was Parker Allington.

JOE: You knew he wasn't?

DAISY: How could he be? Allington's dead. You didn't know he was dead?

JOE: Yes, ma'am. We knew it. . . . One more thing, Miss Wilkers. . . . We've got a description but it's pretty vague.

DAISY: You mean you want to know who he is?

JOE: Yes ma'am.

DAISY: His name's Wilbur Trench.

JOE: What?

DAISY: Used to play bit parts in pictures. . . . Recognized him the minute he came to the door.

A Week's Delights on the Tube

Saturday

3-4:30—BROADWAY TV THEATRE: "George and Margaret," With Ernest Truex, Sylvia Field—(9).

3:45-4—WHAT'S YOUR TROUBLE?—"The Successful Marriage," The Rev. and Mrs. Norman Vincent Peale —(2).

4-4:30—MR. WIZARD, Science, With Don Herbert—(4).

4:30-5—BETWEEN THE LINES: "Are Congressional Investigations Helping Morale of Teachers in New York?"—Robert Morris, Dr. Corliss Lamont, George A. Timone, Prof. H. H. Wilson, Guests—(4).

5-5:30—IT'S A PROBLEM: "New Baby in the Home"— Dr. Helen Wallace, Dr. Emil Piana, Mrs. Clara S. Littledale—(4).

5:30-6—THROUGH THE ENCHANTED GATE: "Easter Parade," With Victor D'Amico—(4).

6:30-7—WHAT IN THE WORLD: Dr. Sherman Lee, Curator of Oriental Art at Cleveland Museum, Guest— (2).

7-7:30—PAUL WHITEMAN TEEN CLUB: With Nancy Lewis—(7).

7:30-8—BEAT THE CLOCK: With Bud Collyer—(2).

7:30-8—JOHNNY JUPITER: Satirical Fantasy, on American Life, as Seen by Inhabitants of Planet Jupiter— (5).

7:30-8—WHAT'S THE BID: Auction-Liberal Bill—(7).

8-9—JACKIE GLEASON SHOW: Jan Peerce, Guest—(2).

8-9—ALL-STAR REVUE: With George Jessel, Eddie Cantor, Fred Allen, Gloria De Haven, Guests—(4).

8:30-9—INTERNATIONAL MOTOR SPORTS SHOW: From Grand Central Palace—(11).

Hit Parade Singers

9-9:30—THIS IS SHOW BUSINESS: Clifton Fadiman, Host; Jacqueline Susann, Nat Cole, Nora Kaye, Guests—(2).

9-10:30—SHOW OF SHOWS: With Sid Caesar, Imogene Coca, Marguerite Piazza, Hostess—(4).

9—LIGHTWEIGHT BOUT: Johnny Gonsalves vs. Virgil Akins, from Chicago's Rainbow Arena—(7).

10:30-11—IT'S NEWS TO ME: Panel Quiz, John Daly—(2).

10:30-11—YOUR HIT PARADE: With Snooky Lanson, Dorothy Collins, June Valli—(4).

10:30-11—AMERICA SPEAKS: "Korean Truce—What It Means to Our Economy"—Ben Limb, Ambassador at Large to the U. N., Guest; Don Passante, Moderator—(9) (Première).

Sunday

11:30 A. M.-1:30—EASTER PARADE, From Park Ave.— (11); 12:30-1:30—Fifth Ave.—(4); 1-2-(2, 7).

3-3:30—VICTORY AT SEA—(4).

3:30-4—YOUTH WANTS TO KNOW: Senator Wayne Morse, Guest—(4).

Sullivan and Dancers

4-4:30—STATE OF THE NATION: Martin P. Durkin, Secretary of Labor—(2).

4:30-6—OMNIBUS: "Everyman," Burgess Meredith; Grandma Moses at Home; "Trip to the Moon"; Other Features; Alistair Cooke, Narrator—(2).

5-5:30—HALL OF FAME THEATRE: "The Other Wise Man," Wesley Addy—(4).

5:30-5:45—SIGHTSEEING WITH SWAYZE—(4) (Première).

6-6:30—YOU ARE THERE: "The Conquest of Mexico" —(2).

6-6:30—MEET THE PRESS: Douglas McKay, Secretary of Interior—(4).

6-7—NEW YORK TIMES YOUTH FORUM: "What Does Religion Mean to Youth?" Dorothy Gordon, Moderator—(5).

6:30-7—SEE IT NOW, With Edward R. Murrow, Narrator —(2).

7:30-8—MR. PEEPERS: Wally Cox—(4).

7:30-8:30—OPERA CAMEOS: "Cavalleria Rusticana," With Rina Telli, Soprano; Martha Lipton, Mezzo-Soprano; Jon Grain, Tenor; Richard Torigi, Baritone —(11).

8-9—TOAST OF THE TOWN: Ed Sullivan; Notre Dame Glee Club; Gracie Fields, Cab Calloway, Others, Guests—(2).

8-9—COMEDY HOUR: Donald O'Connor, Brian Aherne, Vivian Blaine—(4).

9-9:30—FRED WARING SHOW—(2).

9-10—TELEVISION PLAYHOUSE: "Young Lady of Property," Kim Stanley—(4).

9:30-10—KEN MURRAY SHOW—(2).

10-10:30—WEB: "Cry of Trumpets"—(2).

10-10:30—ARTHUR MURRAY SHOW: With Charles Coburn, Lisa Kirk, Christine Jorgensen, Guests—(5).

10:30-11—WHAT'S MY LINE—(2).

10:30-11—FAVORITE STORY—(4).

Monday

7:30-8—HOLLYWOOD SCREEN TEST: Mary Sinclair— (7).

7:30-8:55—BROADWAY TV THEATRE: "Wuthering Heights," With William Prince and Meg Mundy—(9).

8-8:30—GEORGE BURNS AND GRACIE ALLEN—(2).

8-8:30—PAUL WINCHELL-JERRY MAHONEY—(4).

8:30-9—ARTHUR GODFREY TALENT SCOUTS—(2).

8:30-9—JEROME HINES, Basso; Barlow Orchestra—(4).

8:30-9—JOHNS HOPKINS SCIENCE REVIEW: Sir Roger Makins, Guest—(5).

8:30-9:30—METROPOLITAN OPERA JAMBOREE: Symphony Orchestra; Soloists; Deems Taylor, Howard Dietz; Others—(7).

9-9:30—"I LOVE LUCY"; Lucille Ball and Desi Arnaz— (2).

9-9:30—EYEWITNESS—MYSTERY: "Apartment 4-D," With Nita Talbot; Lee Bowman, Host—(4).

9-9:30—NEWS-O-RAMA: Columbia University Forum— (11).

9:30-10—RED BUTTONS SHOW: Gisele MacKenzie, Guest —(2).

9:30-10:30—ROBERT MONTGOMERY PRESENTS: "Second-Hand Sofa," With Ann Rutherford, Leslie Nielsen—(4).

10-11—STUDIO ONE: "Shadow of the Devil," With Mercedes McCambridge and James Dunn—(2).

11-11:15—CHRONOSCOPE: Senator Wayne Morse—(2).

Tuesday

11 A. M.—SENATE INTERNAL SECURITY SUBCOMMITTEE, Investigating Communism in American Education, Senator William Jenner, Chairman; Herbert Philbrick, Witness—(4).

7:30-7:45—THE DINAH SHORE SHOW—(4).

7:45-8—JANE FROMAN'S U.S.A. CANTEEN—(2).

8-9—ERNIE KOVACS SHOW: With Dorothy Richards, Eddie Hatrak, Trigger Lund and Andy McKay—(2).

8-9—STAR THEATRE: With Milton Berle, Cesar Romero, Laraine Day, Kathryn Murray, Guests—(4).

The listing below, based on the program schedule printed by "The New York Times" for the week of April 4, 1953, shows the television highlights a televiewer could have found on CBS (Channel 2), NBC (4), ABC (7) and other channels during a typical week in the 1950s.

8-8:30 – BISHOP FULTON J. SHEEN – (5).

8:30-9 – THE BIG ISSUE: "Should Communists Be Permitted to Teach in Colleges?" – Corliss Lamont, James Burnham – (5).

9-9:30 – CITY HOSPITAL: With Melville Ruick – (2).

9-9:30 – FIRESIDE THEATRE: "Cocoon," Barbara Brown – (4).

9 – FEATHERWEIGHT BOUT: Bill Bossio vs. Miquel Berrios, from Ridgewood Grove, Brooklyn – (7).

9 – PRO-BASKETBALL PLAYOFFS: Knickerbockers vs. Minneapolis Lakers, from 69th Regiment Armory – (11).

9:30-10 – AUTOMOBILE SHOW, from the Waldorf-Astoria Hotel, With Irene Dunne, Hostess – (2).

9:30-10 – CIRCLE THEATRE: "A Slight Case of April," With Hildy Parks and Others – (4).

10-10:30 – DANGER: "Family Jewels," With Gary Merrill – (2).

10-10:30 – TWO FOR THE MONEY, Quiz, Herb Shriner – (4).

10:30-11 – SHOWCASE: "Monkey's Paw," Una Merkel – (2).

11-11:30 – AN EVENING WITH HARRY HERSHFIELD – (7).

Kovacs' Clowns

Wednesday

11 A. M. – SENATE ARMED SERVICES SUBCOMMITTEE, Hearings on Alleged Ammo Shortages in Korea. With Former Secretary of Defense, Robert Lovett, and Assistant Secretary of Defense W. J. McNeil, Witnesses – (4).

7-7:25 – GOVERNOR DEWEY: "New York City's Finances." With Lieut. Gov. Moore, State Comptroller J. Raymond McGovern. Others – (2).

7-7:30 – MARCH OF TIME: "Omaha, Rail Metropolis on the Plains" – (4).

7:15-7:30 – THIS IS CHARLES LAUGHTON: Readings – (11).

7:30-8 – DATE WITH JUDY: With Mary Linn Beller – (7).

7:30-8:55 – BROADWAY TV THEATRE: "Wuthering Heights," With William Prince, Meg Mundy – (9).

7:45-8 – THE PERRY COMO SHOW – (2).

8-9 – ARTHUR GODFREY AND HIS FRIENDS: With Frank Parker, Marion Marlowe, Janette Davis – (2).

8-8:30 – I MARRIED JOAN: With Joan Davis – (4).

8-9 – JUNIOR TOWN MEETING: "Freedom for Enslaved Peoples" – High School Students, Guests – (13).

8:30-9 – MUSIC HALL: Patti Page, Ezio Pinza, Guest – (4).

9-10 – TELEVISION THEATRE: "Next of Kin," With Frederic Tozere, James Daly, Jack Arthur, Pat Ferris – (4).

9-10 – STAGE A NUMBER, Talent Variety Show – (5).

9 – PRO-BASKETBALL PLAYOFFS: Knickerbockers vs. Minneapolis Lakers, from 69th Regiment Armory – (11).

9:30-10 – MAN AGAINST CRIME: With Ralph Bellamy – (2).

10 – FEATHERWEIGHT BOUT: Percy Bassett vs. Davey Gallardo, from Washington – (2).

Godfrey and Tony Marvin

Thursday

11 A. M. – SENATE ARMED SERVICES SUBCOMMITTEE, Hearings on Alleged Ammo Shortages in Korea. With Former Defense Secretary, Robert Lovett, Witness; Senator Margaret Chase Smith, Chairman – (4).

7-7:15 – SAMMY KAYE SHOW: With Jean Martin – (4).

7:30-7:45 – DINAH SHORE SHOW – (4).

7:45-8 – JANE FROMAN'S U.S.A. CANTEEN – (2).

8-8:30 – LIFE WITH LUIGI: Vito Scotti – (2) (Première).

8-8:30 – GROUCHO MARX: "You Bet Your Life" – (4).

8:30-9 – FOUR-STAR PLAYHOUSE: "Dante's Inferno," With Dick Powell, Regis Toomey – (2).

8:30-9 – TREASURY MEN IN ACTION: With Walter Greaza – (4).

8:30-9 – CHANCE OF A LIFETIME: Georgie Price, Guest – (7).

9-9:30 – VIDEO THEATRE: "With Glory and Honor," With Wendell Corey and Others – (2).

9-9:30 – DRAGNET, With Jack Webb – (4).

9 – LIGHT HEAVYWEIGHT BOUT: Chuck Speiser vs. Billy Fifield, from Detroit – (7).

9:30-10 – BIG TOWN: With Patrick McVey, Jane Nigh – (2).

9:30-10 – PLAY: "Just What the Doctor Ordered," With Joanne Dru, Scott Brady, Lisa Ferraday – (4).

9:30-10 – WHAT'S THE STORY: Panel News Quiz – (5).

10-10:30 – MY LITTLE MARGIE: With Gale Storm – (2).

10-10:30 – AUTHOR MEETS THE CRITICS: "Democratic Socialism." Norman Thomas, Prof. Leo Wollman, Michael Straight, Virgilia Peterson, Moderator – (5).

10:30-11 – FOREIGN INTRIGUE: With Jerome Thor – (4).

Groucho and Fenniman

Friday

8-8:30 – MAMA, With Peggy Wood – (2).

8-8:30 – DENNIS DAY SHOW: From Hollywood – (4).

8-8:30 – ADVENTURES OF OZZIE AND HARRIET – (7).

8:30-9 – MY FRIEND IRMA, Marie Wilson, Cathy Lewis – (2).

8:30-9 – THE LIFE OF RILEY, With William Bendix, Marjorie Reynolds and Others – (4).

8:45-9 – RUDOLPH HALLEY REPORTS – (7).

9-9:30 – PLAYHOUSE OF STARS: "The Mirror," With Victor Jory, Ian MacDonald – (2).

9-9:30 – THE BIG STORY: A Reporter's Assignment – (4).

9-9:30 – LIFE BEGINS AT EIGHTY – (5, 13).

9 – PRO-BASKETBALL PLAYOFFS: Knickerbockers vs. Minneapolis Lakers, from the 69th Regiment Armory – (11).

9:30-10 – OUR MISS BROOKS, With Eve Arden – (2).

9:30-10 – THE ALDRICH FAMILY, With Bobby Ellis – (4).

9:30-10 – TALES OF TOMORROW: "Homecoming," With Edith Fellows and Others – (7).

10-10:30 – MR. AND MRS. NORTH: With Richard Denning, Barbara Britton – (2).

10 – MIDDLEWEIGHT BOUT: Jimmy Beau vs. Randy Sandy, from the St. Nicholas Arena – (4).

10-10:30 – TWENTY QUESTIONS: Blanche Thebom, Guest – (5).

Signatures of the '50s

"Ding Dong School's" Miss Frances clangs the school bell.

Loretta Young ends by reading aloud some homely wisdom.

Betty Furness says goodnight for her new refrigerator.

A spotlighted Durante says "Goodnight, Mrs. Calabash."

Red Buttons soft-shoes it offstage to his "Ho-Ho Song."

"Peace," says Dave Garroway, signing off for "Today."

Having advised her listeners to "See the U.S.A. in your Chevrolet," Dinah Shore ends her show by blowing a big, smacking kiss.

Picture Credits

Text Credits

Acknowledgments

The editors of 1940-1950: The Patriotic Tide *wish to thank the following persons and institutions for their assistance:*

Joseph Avery, Archives, Washington National Record Center; Dany Barker, New Orleans; Paul Bonner, The Condé Nast Publications, Inc., New York City; Sarah Boynton, LIFE Picture Collection, New York City; Mrs. Ruth P. Braun, Chief Librarian, *The Detroit News;* Burton Historical Collection, The Detroit Public Library; Greg Carpenter, Photographer, *Orlando Sentinel,* Orlando, Florida; Romeo Carraro, Head Librarian, *The Los Angeles Times;* The Honorable Richard H. Cooper, Orlando, Florida; Jim Coughlin, Orlando, Florida; Virginia Daiker, Prints and Photographs Division, Library of Congress; James H. Davis, Western History Division, Denver Public Library; Frank Driggs, New York City; Eugene Ferrara, New York *Daily News;* Sue Flanagan, Institute of Texan Cultures at San Antonio; Hugh R. Foley, Principal, Hollywood High School, Hollywood, California; Tommy Giles, Montgomery, Alabama; Leonard Huber, New Orleans; Mrs. Joye Jordan, North Carolina Museum of History, Raleigh; Frank Kavaler, The Curtis Publishing Co., Philadelphia; Labor History Archives, Wayne State University, Detroit; John W. Lewis Jr., Lafayette, Louisiana; William H. McDonald, Editor, *The Montgomery Advertiser,* Montgomery, Alabama; Mrs. Maier, Archives, Louisiana State University Library, Baton Rouge; Dr. William Mason, History Division, Los Angeles County Museum of Natural History; Bill Matthews, City of Miami Beach News Bureau; Michigan Historical Commission Archives, Lansing; Jane Milligan, The Saturday Evening Post Co., New York City; Joseph Molloy, Librarian, *The Philadelphia Inquirer;* Allen Morris, Florida State University, Tallahassee; Mrs. Grace Mullins, *The Galveston Daily News;* Sol Novin, Culver Pictures, New York City; Melvin Parks, Museum of the City of New York; Margot P. Pearsall, Curator, Social History Division, Detroit Historical Museum; Mrs. M. R. Pirnie, Montgomery, Alabama; Winthrop Sears Jr., Associate Archivist, Ford Archives, Henry Ford Museum, Dearborn; Sy Seidman, New York City; Russell Shaw, *Corpus Christi Caller-Times;* Dorothy Shipp, Chief, Photo Negative Files, *Fort Worth Star Telegram;* Mildred Simpson, Librarian, Academy of Motion Picture Arts and Sciences, Los Angeles; Ray Stuart, R. R. Stuart Collection, Los Angeles; Mrs. Betty Sprigg, Audio-Visual Division, Department of Defense; Richard W. Taylor, Research Staff, Photo Library, United Press International, New York City; Lieutenant Colonel Douglas B. Tucker, Information Officer, U.S. Army Infantry Center, Fort Benning, Georgia; Jerome A. Waterman, Maas Brothers Department Store, Tampa; David Wilson, Pix Inc., New York City.

The editors of 1950-1960: Shadow of the Atom *wish to thank the following persons and institutions for their assistance:*

Mrs. Eve Bayne, Chief Librarian, Dell Publishing Co. Inc., New York City; Ruth P. Braun, Chief Librarian, *The Detroit News;* Bill Bridges, Los Angeles; Sid Caesar, Los Angeles; Fred Coe, New York City; Frank Driggs, New York City; Gabe Essoe, Publicist, Walt Disney Productions, Burbank, California; Mark Greenberg, MacFadden-Bartell Corp., New York City; Garth Hamby, The Coca-Cola Company, Atlanta, Georgia; Stephen Holden, New York City; Roy L. King, Chief Librarian, *St. Louis Post-Dispatch;* Lawrence Lariar, Freeport, New York; Mitchell Lewis, McLendon Corp., Dallas; Jack Meltzer, New York City; Joseph Molloy, *Philadelphia Inquirer;* Joseph Nettis, Philadelphia; Mrs. Pat Pappas, *Playboy* magazine, Chicago; Mildred Simpson, Librarian, Academy of Motion Picture Arts and Sciences, Los Angeles; Tony Spina, Chief Photographer, *Detroit Free Press;* Ty Triplett, The Five-State Edsell Club, Grosse Pointe, Michigan; Leigh Weiner, Los Angeles.

Bibliography

Allen, Frederick Lewis, *The Big Change, 1900-1950.* Bantam Books, 1965.

Anderson, Jack, and Ronald W. May, *McCarthy: The Man, The Senator, The "Ism."* The Beacon Press, 1952.

Becker, Stephen, *Comic Art in America.* Simon & Schuster, 1959.

Bellaire, Arthur, *TV Advertising.* Harper & Bros., 1959.

Biddle, Daniel, *In Brief Authority.* Doubleday & Co., 1962.

Block, Haskell M., and Robert G. Sheed, *Masters of Modern Drama.* Random House, Inc., 1962.

Blum, Daniel:
    A Pictorial History of the American Theatre. Greenberg: Publisher, 1951.
    Pictorial History of Television. Chilton Co., 1959.

Bogart, Leo, *The Age of Television.* Frederick Ungar Publishing Co., 1956.

Burns, James MacGregor, *Roosevelt: The Lion and the Fox.* Harcourt, Brace and World, Inc., 1956.

Carlson, John Roy, *Under Cover.* E. P. Dutton & Co., Inc., 1943.

Ewen, David, *Complete Book of the American Musical Theater.* Henry Holt and Co., 1958.

Farago, Ladislas, *The Broken Seal.* Random House, Inc., 1967.

Friendly, Fred W., *Due to Circumstances Beyond Our Control. . . .* Random House, Inc., 1967.

Friendly, Fred W. and Edward R. Murrow, eds., *See It Now.* Simon & Schuster, Inc., 1955.

Goldman, Eric F.:
    The Crucial Decade: America 1945-1960. Random House, Inc., 1960.
    The Crucial Decade—And After. Random House, Inc., 1960.

Goodman, Jack, ed., *While You Were Gone.* Simon & Schuster, 1946.

Green, Abel, and Joe Laurie Jr., *Show Biz.* Henry Holt and Co., 1951.

Guiles, F. L., *Norma Jean.* McGraw-Hill, Inc., 1969.

Higham, Charles, and Joel Greenberg, *Hollywood in the Forties.* A. S. Barnes & Co., 1968.

Hoehling, A. A.:
    Home Front, U.S.A. Thomas Y. Crowell Co., 1966.
    The Week Before Pearl Harbor. W. W. Norton & Company, 1963.

Hough, Major Frank O., *The Island War.* J. B. Lippincott Co., 1947.

Kendrick, Alexander, *Prime Time.* Little, Brown and Co., 1967.

King, Martin Luther, Jr., *Stride Toward Freedom.* Ballantine Books, Inc., 1958.

Lord, Walter, *Day of Infamy.* Holt, Rinehart and Winston, 1957.

Martin, Ralph, *The G.I. War.* Little, Brown & Co., 1967.

Millis, Walter, *This Is Pearl!* William Morrow & Co., 1947.

Morgenstern, George, *Pearl Harbor.* The Devin-Adair Co., 1947.

Moss, Norman, *Men Who Play God.* Harper & Row, 1968.

Myers, Debs, Jonathan Kilbourn and Richard Harrity, eds., *Yank—The G.I. Story of the War.* Duell, Sloan & Pearce, 1947.

Nelson, Benjamin, *Tennessee William:. The Man and His Work.* Ivan Obolensky Inc., 1961.

Prideaux, Tom, *World Theatre in Pictures.* Greenberg: Publisher, 1953.

Rodgers and Hammerstein Fact Book. Richard Rodgers & Oscar Hammerstein II, 1955.

Rovere, Richard H., *Senator Joe McCarthy.* Harcourt, Brace and Co., 1959.

Sann, Paul, *Fads, Follies and Delusions of the American People.* Crown Publishers, Inc., 1967.

Serling, Rod, *Patterns.* Simon & Schuster, Inc., 1957.

Settel, Irving and William Laas, *A Pictorial History of Television.* Grosset & Dunlap, Inc., 1969.

Shaw, Arnold, *Sinatra.* Holt, Rinehart and Winston, 1968.

Shepley, James R., and Clay Blair Jr., *The Hydrogen Bomb.* David McKay Company, Inc., 1954.

Shulman, Arthur and Roger Youman, *How Sweet It Was.* Bonanza Books, 1966.

Toland, John, *But Not in Shame.* Random House, Inc., 1961.

Whitehead, Don, *The FBI Story.* Random House, Inc., 1956.

Whitman, Alden R. and *The New York Times, Portrait: Adlai E. Stevenson.* Harper & Row, 1965.

Wohlstetter, Roberta, *Pearl Harbor, Warning and Decision.* Stanford University Press, 1962.

Index